She THINKS LIKE A *CEO*

 LEVERAGING TECHNOLOGY FOR TODAY'S WOMEN LEADERS

Carol J. Dunlop, Renee Coakley, Selena Teems, Lori A. Manns, Nadine Mullings, Tina Bolden, Alicia Couri

What the authors clients are saying . . .

Carol J. Dunlop:

Before working with **Carol**, I did not have a viable and functional website. She totally created and designed a top of the line site that clearly depicted my developing brand. I have received many compliments on the design of my site and how easy it is to navigate. Carol is very knowledgeable and resourceful with a vast degree of creative and marketing skills. I was involved in several of her courses which gave me the foundation to move forward in developing my niche as well as my brand. *The Authority Blogging Course* was powerful. Although I had adequate blog content, I am now better equipped to position and maximize my content. She is prepared to meet the challenges of today in the media and marketing arena taking you to the next level.

~ *Barbra Gentry-Pugh*

Tina Bolden:

Tina Bolden is a dedicated, seasoned Tax Advisor who screams passion when Speaking Tax! She knows her numbers and she's willing to share her expertise and knowledge with others. She is invaluable. I'd recommend her for clients with stock options, entrepreneurs, small businesses, and shareholders. She does complete and accurate work!

~ *Fran H.*

Ms. Tina has been my "Tax-Smart Wealth Strategist for over 10 years, and she has been a significant value add over the years. Not only does she make sure that I understand how to provide her supporting documents, she reviews the tax returns in detail in order to avoid an audit. I am a loyal client based on her knowledge and expertise. I'd recommend her for small businesses owners and those who want to understand what they are doing with their personal and business taxes.

~ *Ms. Barbara D.*

Selena Teems:

Successful YOU!™, by **Selena Teems**, has taken what could have been an overwhelming experience and mapped it out in manageable steps. I am more informed about the self publishing process and the options available to me as an aspiring author.

~ *Maricely Rodríguez*

What the authors clients are saying . . .

Lori A. Manns:

I'm so glad I joined the Trailblazer CEO Masterclass and invested in myself through Lori's training class. This class helped me to identify the marketing strategies to attract new clients. After implementing some of the strategies I learned, I signed two contracts that resulted in $20K and another $10K in my sales funnel. I would definitely recommend working with Lori if you want to get more clients and grow your sales.

Patryce Curtis
PC Eval Consulting

Nadine Mullings:

I reached out to **Nadine** to talk about better connecting my heart and voice in my messaging. I was doing "it" according to the prevailing influencer and expert recommendations. And even though I was communicating it felt like I was holding back on my heart and what I really needed to share. I worked with Nadine in a single, private session and made great strides. Then, our small but mighty team met with Nadine to create a 90-day approach to incorporate my work and our team's vision. If you are an entrepreneur and woman of faith or deep spiritual connection needing marketing support, Nadine is a business woman and coach who can assist brilliantly.

~ Sarah Boxx
Owner of Sarah Box, LLC

Nadine's Mastermind gave me a new perspective on how I approach my business. I learned the importance of business care and self-care, which were two struggles for me, so now I'm consistently taking time with God, taking time for myself, and this has helped me to activate my faith in my business and my personal life.

~ Melissa Hinton
Owner of The Hinton Agency

Thank you Sponsors

Angela R. Lewis, CPA: 10 Glenlake Dr Suite 130, Atlanta, GA. 30328, NRV Financial Services, LLC Atlanta, GA., www.nrvfs.com, (770) 609-7272, www.linkedin.com/in/AngelaRLewisCPA

April N. West: 7010 Biltmore Trace, Lithonia, GA 30058, Gail M. Frazier Legacy Foundation, Atlanta, GA., www.gmflegacy.org 404-913-9392, www.linkedin.com/in/AprilNWest

Brenda R. Coone: P O Box 680943, Prattville, AL 36068, MsCraftprincess Designs, Prattville, Alabama, www.mscraftprincessdesigns.com, (334) 322-0122, www.facebook.com/mscraftprincess

Carolvita R. Johnson: 309 Lehigh Circle, Clyo GA. 31303, A'TIVLORAC Unique Boutique, 712 North Laurel Street, 300 #1014, Springfield, GA 31329, www.marykay.com/CRJohnson1 1.912.521.5026, www.facebook.com/Ativlorac

Evonya Easley: 212 Arthur Drive McDonough, GA 30252, Love E Fashion, Atlanta, GA., loveefashion.com, 404-908-7997, www.instagram.com/styledbylovee

Fred Blain: Gospel Highway Eleven Online, 2471 W Cheltenham Ave., Ste D-120, Wyncote, PA 19095, lamontmedia7@gmail.com, www.mygospelhighway11.com, 267-423-4411, FB Gospel Highway 11

Jennifer M. Coffee: 5 Dunwoody Park suite 115, Atlanta, GA 30338 JStar Studio Salon   Atlanta, Georgia   www.jstarstudiosalon. com   404-836-3101 www.instagram.com/jstarstudiosalon

Dr. Julee Hafner: 2772 Galindo Circle, Melbourne, FL 32940 DrJuleeHafner.com, Melbourne, FL, www.drjuleehafner.com 321-720-7280, www.LinkedIn.com/in/DrJuleeHafner

Kitura Smith: 5341 Rolling Meadow Drive, Powder Springs, GA 30127, All About The Mini's, Atlanta, Georgia, www.chefkitura.com 770-800-8219, www.instagram.com/chefkitura

Patryce Curtis: 4245 Trillium Wood Trail, Snellville, GA 30039, PC Eval Consulting, LLC, Atlanta, GA., www.pcevalconsulting.com 470-867-6977, www.facebook.com/pcevalconsulting

Thank you Sponsors

Sharon Reid: 4153-C Flat Shoals Parkway, Suites 330-H, Decatur, GA 30034, Three Hearts One Beat, Inc., Decatur, GA., theeheartlady.com 470-314-0772, www.facebook.com/TheeHeartLady/

Siera Suazo: Siera Project Co., LLC, New Jersey, sieraproject.co, (609) 775-9142, www.linkedin.com/company/siera-project-co

Tamisa S Lundy: 1102 Whispering Oaks Dr. Brunswick Ga. 31520, Sister's Keep-Her, Brunswick, Georgia, tamisas-store-2.creator-spring.com, 623-330-1347, www.facebook.com/tamisa.lundy

Tisha Smith-Allen: LUXE Image Agency, Atlanta, GA, 3628 Satellite Blvd #957132 Duluth GA 30096, marykay.com/iamtishaLUXE, 470.280.6714, @iamtishaLUXE

Vicki Wright Hamilton: 780 Glen Royal Drive Roswell, GA 30076, VWH Consulting, Roswell, GA, VickiWrightHamilton.com, 770-230-5337, @Vickiwhamilton

She Thinks Like a CEO:
Leveraging Technology for Today's Women Leaders
© 2023 Creative Services International, Inc.

First published by Creative Services International, Inc.

Printed in the United States of America
Creative Services International, Inc.
2615 George Busbee Pkwy
Suite 11-154
Kennesaw, GA 30144-4981

csicorporation.com

Book and Cover design by CSI, Inc

Table of Contents

Dedication

I dedicate this book to my wonderful husband, #BFF4Life, and super duper supporter, Alvin Dunlop.

~ Carol J. Dunlop

I would like to thank my family for being a constant source of love and support. I Love you Calbert, Kennedy and Christian.

~ Renee Coakley

I dedicate this book to ALL the women who have a vision to grow a successful and sustainable business that makes a difference in the world and glorifies God. Know and understand you have been given the desire for a reason, you just need to TRUST and BELIEVE anything is possible with God!

~ Nadine Mullings

I dedicate this book to my mother for being a supportive prayer warrior for me and my entrepreneurial endeavors. I also dedicate this book to the women entrepreneurs who joined as partners and early supporters, may your businesses experience exponential success.

~ Lori A. Manns

Introduction

As a female entrepreneur, you may find yourself constantly using phrases like "I'm on my hustle" or "I'm out here, grinding," even if your business is well-established. You likely desire more of everything, from time, to acquiring leads, to sales, to bringing on team members, to cashflow, to sleep.

Despite your hard work, you may feel like your business isn't growing as fast as you want it to. This isn't your fault. Women entrepreneurs face more barriers to growth than their male counterparts, despite launching businesses at record rates.

If your business:

- generates less than $143,431 annually
- you have difficulty obtaining a traditional business loan
- you run a solo enterprise and feel overwhelmed
- or you believe that a mentor could help you progress faster . . .

you are not alone! These are some of the most significant challenges that female entrepreneurs, especially those from minority backgrounds, face.

The 2019 State of Women-Owned Businesses report, commissioned by American Express, found that women encounter more obstacles than their male counterparts when launching and expanding their businesses. The study also revealed that the number of women-owned businesses increased by 21% between 2014 and the report's publication date, with women of color owning firms that grew at twice that rate (43%). African American/Black women-owned businesses experienced even faster growth, increasing by 50%.

However, the average revenue of women-of-color-owned businesses decreased during the same period, except for Asian women-owned businesses. Despite these challenges, female entrepreneurs can overcome them and achieve success.

"Doubling down and working longer hours isn't the solution," as a study by Ohio State University and Mayo Clinic demonstrated that women who work more than 40 hours per week have a higher risk of developing arthritis and diabetes. Women who work over 50 hours per week are also more likely to develop heart disease or cancer (except for skin cancer).

So, how can female founders establish, expand, and grow their businesses without working excessively long hours to achieve their income goals?

In today's business environment, technology is essential and can be the key to keeping your business afloat. By using technology, you can work smarter instead of harder, allowing you to focus on growing your business. Even if you're new to the business world or looking to expand, the right technology can help you increase your earning potential.

For example, **a single mom** juggling a side hustle and a day job can leverage the right hardware and software combination to save time. **A full-time entrepreneur** can use marketing and sales automation tools to streamline their lead generation and sales process. **A small business owner** can utilize the right software suite to gain visibility into their business's performance over the next 5 years, allowing them to make informed decisions today. And **a CEO** looking to take their business to the next level can invest in enterprise-level tech to manage their exponential growth.

Regardless of your business's current size or stage, technology can help you achieve your goals.

In this book, you'll learn from dynamic women of color entrepreneurs who are leading the way in their respective industries and using innovative technology to succeed. They share their tips, tricks, and hacks that have helped them rise above their peers and achieve extraordinary accomplishments.

MEET THE AUTHORS OF "SHE THINKS LIKE A CEO:"

Carol J. Dunlop is the lead author of this book. She is known as The Online WOW! Strategist and is a 6X Best-Selling author. Carol and her husband, Alvin have run their company for 29 years. She'll be showing you how to use automated systems to create a sales funnel full of warm prospects waiting to buy your products and services. No more unpredictable revenue!

Renee Coakley is co-owner of "The Closing Academy." She is a powerhouse in the sales industry. She teaches entrepreneurs and sales professionals how to sell. She believes that "Sales is a Teachable Skill." Renee will detail how she used an image creation platform to surge her business's sales.

Selena Teems is a consultant who is assisting her growing tribe of self-published authors and the freelancers who serve them. Read her chapter to learn how she successfully forces Facebook to feed her business with qualified leads continuously.

Do you want more visibility for your business or personal brand? **Alicia Couri** is the one to learn from. A personal branding coach, Kolbe Certified™ Consultant, and media personality, Alicia shares the tactics she uses to leverage the power of multi-streaming video to increase her and her client's authority and cash flow.

Dr. Lori A. Manns is an award-winning business coach and strategist who consults and trains entrepreneurs on best practices to master their marketing and increase sales as well as secure sponsorships. In her chapter, Dr. Lori will share how to utilize video marketing to grow your brand, become an authority in your niche, and elevate your sales.

Nadine Mullings, whose known for her B.E.S.T. Marketing System™, specializes in helping female coaches and consultants succeed in four key areas of their marketing. In her chapter, you'll discover how scheduling systems give her and her clients greater efficiency and less stress!

Tina R. Bolden, EA, MST, MBA is a Tax and Wealth Advisor; she helps her clients keep more of the money they make! Ms. Tina will share a simple hack for maximizing her client's tax deductions and increasing their profitability.

You don't have to go through this alone! Even better, you now have access to the resources that can guide you in the right direction. This book was created for you, with each contributing author eager to assist you in discovering how to utilize the necessary tools to achieve success in both your business and personal life. The authors are here to help you solidify your brand, generate more income, and regain some much-needed personal time!

"Some failure in life is inevitalbe. It is impossible to live without failing at something, unless you live so cautiously that you might as well not have lived at all—in which case, you fail by default."

~J.K. Rowling

Automate Your Lead Generation and Turn Leads Into Clients by Leveraging THIS Technology Tool

Over **75% of email revenue** is generated by triggered campaigns rather than one-size-fits-all campaigns. Email marketing is one of the most effective ways you can share your message, sell your services, and build a relationship with your clients. In fact, companies who send automated emails are **133%** more likely to send relevant messages that correspond with a customer's purchase cycle.

Active Campaign is an email marketing, marketing automation, sales automation, and CRM software platform for small-to-mid-sized businesses. *Active Campaign* gives you the email marketing, marketing automation, and CRM tools you need to create great customer experiences.

Automated email campaigns account for 21% of email marketing revenue. **94% of Internet users use email.** Therefore, marketing through email allows you to reach a great deal of Internet users even if they are not on social media. Furthermore, a survey found that an astounding 75% of adult online users say email marketing is actually their preferred marketing method!

If you're not already utilizing email marketing, it's definitely something you should consider in order to reach a wider audience and strengthen your brand's relationship with current clients. Another benefit of email marketing is that it's incredibly easy to track your ROI.

Carol J. Dunlop has twenty-nine years of entrepreneurial experience. She is an 6X Amazon Best-selling author. She teaches purpose driven entrepreneurs to convert marketing into money using their website as their hub while leveraging technology.

Sit back and quickly learn about a technology that can make a difference in your business. Carol J. Dunlop will share how leveraging an email marketing platform and other technologies can help you launch, grow, or scale, and achieve a greater level of success!

A Conversation with Carol J. Dunlop

The technology platform that I use in my business that really made a difference for me is *Active Campaign.* Using this software, I am able to automate many of my business processes.

We only have so much time during the day, and I would rather spend it doing client work, meeting new clients, or prospecting than I would doing "busy work."

Automation plays a key role in client acquisition. Having an opt-in (ethical bribe or Lead Magnet) on your website to capture the name and email address of people who visit is crucial to building your business. You've heard the old saying, "The money is in the list." It's the truth. Without a list of potential buyers who you can touch or connect with regularly, you don't actually have a business.

To tell you the truth, I am not sitting in front of my website waiting for someone to land on it and say, "Hey, do you want this freebie?" *Active Campaign* empowers my website to capture leads so I can then convert them into paying clients.

When a potential client lands on my website, a pop-up appears and urges them to enter their name and email address. In exchange, they receive something of value. They are then put into an automation sequence where they receive a set number of emails that leads them to purchase automatically.

This process lets my web visitors know that they're in the right place to get their problem solved. It solidifies my authority, showcases my expertise, and provides a solution, and I'm not even there. That is what automation can do for you, and it's just a small part of the process.

What was hard before I leveraged this technology

I tried different CRMs (customer relationship management) before settling on *Active Campaign*.

Before, I could see how many people opened the email and how many people clicked, but I wasn't able to see who opened it and what time they did it. There weren't any reports that showed me who was engaged and who was simply squatting on my list.

I felt that I was missing a vital piece of information because I wasn't sure if the content I was providing was actually doing the job I intended or that the client needed.

I am an information seeker and problem solver. I knew there had to be a better way of learning what I needed to know about my audience.

What changed for me implementing this technology

Now that I'm using *Active Campaign*, I am able to see who **opened** the emails, who **clicks** the links that lead back to my website, **how many times** they visit, and **when** they purchase. This type of information is invaluable when you are trying to figure out the best or next product or service to offer.

I can do more in less time. I can set up sales funnels that involve automatic delivery of emails that go out while I'm working on other client projects. Within the sales funnel, when someone purchases, they are automatically tagged so they don't receive any more buying notices.

> **"New clients are automatically sent through the onboarding process, and potential clients are sent to my scheduling software.**

New clients are automatically sent through the onboarding process, and potential clients are sent to my scheduling software. All of this happens without me having to physically do it myself. That is the power of automating your business processes using *Active Campaign*.

Three pivotal reasons why every entrepreneur and especially female entrepreneurs should work with a coach, hire a consultant, or have a mentor

It's important to have a coach, consultant, or mentor. You are good at what you do, but you are not good or even great at everything. There are many processes, techniques, and strategies that are needed to make your business work successfully, and you don't have to do them all or even know them all. Hiring a coach allows you to concentrate and perfect what you do best, while learning how to delegate what you don't like or don't want to do.

> **"One of the best reasons to hire a coach, secure a mentor, or bring in a consultant is that you don't know what you don't know.**

One of the best reasons to hire a coach, secure a mentor, or bring in a consultant is that you don't know what you don't know. Sometimes, you just need a second set of eyes or ears to tweak what you're doing or to simply let you know it's time to move on or level up.

How this technology will make a difference in your business

Using *Active Campaign* and truly embracing all it has to offer will change the way you do business. You don't have to glue yourself to the computer or to your desk to stalk your website to see when potential clients stop by.

Most people don't buy the first time they meet or encounter you. It takes, on average, **21 touches** before a person purchases. These touches may include reading an email, watching your video, listening to your podcast, or reading your blog. Even if you are a one-woman show, you don't have time to look at every click or diagnose each stat.

Active Campaign does all of that for you. They have a reports section where you can pull just about any type of report and locate the data and information on your audience that is most important to you.

Why you should consider adding this technology platform to help you launch, grow, or scale your business

The data you glean from *Active Campaign* empowers you to make informed and strategic decisions regarding what products to offer or retire, which communications are working or tanking, and whether or not your messages are resonating with your audience. All of this information saves you valuable time you can dedicate elsewhere in your business or into getting your life back.

Challenges I can help you avoid

I help my clients avoid wasting time and money with products and services that don't work for them or that give them headaches instead of income.

How you can go further faster

The right technology can help you change the world and make life easier for you, your business, and your family.

The wrong technology can waste your time and money and cause you to second-guess everything.

I'm here to steer you in the right direction to the technology that works for you so you can have the freedom and money to do what you want to do in life and for your business.

The benefits of leveraging this technology

Time is a fleeting, non-renewable resource. Once it's gone, it's gone, never to return. Managing your list and being able to not only relate to your audience but connect with them on a regular basis is the key to business success.

Active Campaign keeps you on track for communicating with your audience. Plus, it lets you know what's working and what's not, so you don't waste time, but instead **gain back time** by sending the **right** message to the **right** audience at the **right** time.

A successful outcome

Several of my clients are actually authors in this book. They trust me to let them know about great resources. *Active Campaign* is a resource that I teach, promote, and talk about every chance I get.

Nadine Mullings, a co-author, client, and colleague, informed me she was searching for a better mail list provider because she wanted to know more about how her audience was interacting with her content. Of course, I immediately shared my knowledge about *Active Campaign*.

Since she started using *Active Campaign*, she has been able to revamp her offerings and has since created her quarterly "Power of ..." brunches that are often times sold out. She used the information she gained via the reporting in *Active Campaign* to get clued in on what her audience wanted so she could provide exactly what they needed.

Things were challenging for me, too, until I leveraged this technology

Marketing, in general, was a challenge for me, but I knew it had to be done. I used *Active Campaign* to figure out the best time to send emails, what subjects were of interest, and what products would sell.

Now, I use *Active Campaign's* reporting system to see where my profit areas are and use that to wash, rinse, and repeat what works.

A lesson I learned

I've learned that people don't know what they need, but they do know what they want. If you sell them what they want and provide what they need inside the package, you'll have a winning solution.

Questions you should ask yourself . . .

The most important question to ask yourself is, **WHO** are you providing solutions for and **WHAT** is the problem they are looking to solve?

Once you know the answers, you will be able to provide the right solution to the people who will pay you to get it.

My recommendation

My recommendation is to start using *Active Campaign* today! Don't wait because your audience is in pain and looking for your solution, even as you are reading.

If you don't provide what they are looking for, they will go elsewhere.

Active Campaign lets you know if you are reaching the right people with a message that resonates with them, so you aren't wasting time and money guessing what is working and what isn't.

Connect with me. I can help you!

The best way for you to know if Active Campaign will work for you is to have a conversation with me and discuss your needs (and wants) for your business. Go to **www.csicorporation.com/vc** to set up a time to have a conversation with me.

A bit about me and the difference I can make working with you

My name is Carol J. Dunlop. I'm the Online WOW! strategist. I teach entrepreneurs how to covert marketing into money. I love working with women entrepreneurs, but I also work with a few great men.

The one big problem that I specialize in solving is getting entrepreneurs to realize that they need to market their business. You **can't afford not to market** your business these days, in this digital economy. Even the smallest business with the smallest staff can be found through the use of technology and can excel well past their goals, but you have to be out there.

By working with me, I will empower you to choose the marketing strategy that you love and to keep doing it until you know it like the back of your hand. I have found that if you actually practice the marketing strategy that you love, you will excel. Talking, creating videos, or writing; it doesn't matter. You will keep doing it, and you will get better at it, and you will be at ease with it. You'll also be able to connect with your audience. It's imperative that entrepreneurs, especially women entrepreneurs, are able to do that, because we always have the issue with thinking that we aren't good enough or don't know enough.

None of that matters when you feel comfortable with what you're doing.

I empower you to be able to take the marketing strategy you love and use it so that you can secure the clients that you want to work with. It's imperative that you figure out what marketing strategy you want to and like to do and then do it.

> **"Working with me, I will empower you to choose the marketing strategy that you love and to keep doing it until you know it like the back of your hand.**

My ideal client that I totally love to work with is a woman who's approaching the best years of her life, after 45. You're doing the things that you want to do. You're making a difference. Your kids are probably grown or half-grown and on their way out of the house. Maybe you've been married or even divorced. You know what you need, but you don't know how to accomplish it. I love working with entrepreneurs who know what they want to do but feel that technology is getting in the way.

What's different about me is that I am in the over-50 age group. Most people around my age think that the only people who are not technologically challenged are the millennials. Although Millennials grew up with the technology that everyone's using now, I'm here to show you that even baby boomers, like myself, can use technology to their benefit.

Yes, you, too, can use technology to get in front of your ideal clients.

The problems my company helps solve

My company solves the problem entrepreneurs have of looking at technology and getting an instant headache from it, throwing up their hands and saying, "I can't do this." I empower you to say, "Yes! I can do this."

As I said in the beginning, you must embrace technology. But you don't have to do everything yourself. You can hire people to help you, but you must know the power of technology and how to use it in your business in order to move forward. You don't have to be a tech expert, but you do have to know the tech that can really save you time in your daily life and business.

How I overcame a challenging stage in my business

I struggled with marketing. Before I became an expert at marketing, I continually asked myself, how do I do this? What do I do? I knew that my background in marketing my personal training business could help me.

When I started that personal training company, social media was just beginning. I used social media as my main marketing vehicle media because I didn't want to take money from my main business to invest in marketing, and it was free. I learned how to use social media, email marketing, and content marketing. I then incorporated those techniques into what I'm doing now.

People started asking me, "Carol, how did you get all those people to follow you? How do you know about social media and email marketing, using video, and other content to get clients?"

I had been marketing my training business for over 10 years and saw success, but I needed a change. When I re-launched CSI, I was in growth mode.

I went back to web design, but this time, I brought in social media, content marketing, and email marketing. Now, people were asking me to teach them how to market their business like I did mine.

Clients wanted to incorporate functionality into their websites that they didn't even know existed. I was able to accommodate what they wanted because I understood technology and how it worked to attract clients. I had done it for myself, and now I could do it for them.

What did you learn from this chapter or this book? Feel free to use the #SheThinksLikeACEO hashtag and let us know. On the two pages following this chapter, you'll be able to record your thoughts and Aha's.

Carol J. Dunlop, The Online WOW! Strategist and 6X Amazon Best-selling author, influential podcast host, and expert event producer, teaches Purpose Driven Entrepreneurs to convert marketing into money using their WOW! Website so that they can live the lifestyle they want. Carol's clients hail from cities across the U.S.A., the U.K., New Zealand, and Australia. Carol is currently working to promote the Best-Selling books, Influential podcasts, and Expert summits that her clients are creating.

Website: www.csicorporation.com
Location: Atlanta, Georgia
Facebook: www.facebook.com/csicorporation
Twitter: twitter.com/csicorporation
LinkedIN: www.linkedin.com/in/coachauthordesigner
              www.instagram.com/csicorporation

Use this area to journal your thoughts
surrounding your Aha's from this chapter.

Use this area to journal your thoughts
surrounding your Aha's from this chapter.

"What would you do if you knew you could not fail?"

~Unknown

Catapault Your Business With This Easy-To-Use Graphic Solution

Have you heard the saying, "A picture is worth a thousand words?" If you want your business to stand out from your competitors, then you need to add graphic design to your marketing strategies.

Canva is an online platform and app that has pre-made templates to help even a non-designer to easily create a variety of engaging graphics to share and use in their marketing.

You might be saying, "But I'm not a designer."

You can design beautiful graphics in minutes, and it will be content that will encourage prospects to become customers. High-quality visuals increase viewer interaction and can accentuate your marketing efforts across all channels.

Have you ever needed a simple tweak to a graphic, and no one was around? Have you tried hiring freelancers or outsourced graphic designers, and they ghosted you, just when you needed to have a marketing piece that you did not know how to make yourself? Whether you need a social media image, a flyer, a stunning presentation, sales piece, or video, the *Canva* platform empowers you to get it done! This secret weapon will help you take back control in your business.

Renee Coakley is an accomplished sales and marketing expert operating a six-figure business that continues to earn profit. She teaches entrepreneurs and sales professionals how to improve sales by leveraging the power of good graphic design in their marketing strategy, increasing visibility and brand awareness. According to Renee Coakley, "Nothing will make you stand out from the crowd more than well-executed branding."

Sit back and quickly learn about a technology that can make a difference in your business.

Renee Coakley will share how leveraging the *Canva* platform can help you launch, grow, or scale and achieve a greater level of success!

A Conversation with Renee Coakley

The technology platform I use that made a difference in my business

We knew that we were going to need to use graphics in order to help promote our business and help promote our services, so one of the platforms that we decided to use was **Canva.** Canva has made a huge difference in our business. There were many times that we needed to advertise a sale or make a social media post, but we didn't have time to always meet with the graphic designer, and we needed a professional level graphic. On an everyday basis, we needed social media posts, sales flyers, and event flyers. *Canva* became our go to platform to use to create these graphics.

What was hard before I leveraged this technology

There were many times that we needed graphics done, and we hired graphic designers, and we had to wait days for them to come back with a draft. Then when they did come back with a draft, a lot of times we had to make revisions, or there were things that we were not happy with as far as the graphics. *Canva* has allowed us to be able to hop on the platform, make the graphics that we needed to make, and then not have to worry about the length of time that it takes in order to get the graphics back or have the graphics approved. With *Canva*, we're able to just hop online, choose a template, make a graphic really quickly and post it on social media or even send it to the printer to be printed.

What changed for me implementing this technology

Implementing this technology has brought a significant amount of exposure. I have been able to create attractive thumbnails for our YouTube channel, as well as headers and banners for LinkedIn, Facebook, and Twitter. I have effortlessly produced infographics, lead magnets, and graphics for our landing pages. This technology has made the creation of graphics easier, but it has also allowed us to deliver bite-sized content that can be consumed quickly by our audience. It has also allowed us to save money, time, and to be able to have an overall professional cohesive look. In short, it made our business life easier.

How this technology will make a difference in your business

Canva is a valuable tool that has significantly impacted my business operations. Its user-friendly platform, abundant templates, and extensive graphics library have enabled me to save time and streamline my content creation process. While it doesn't replace the expertise of a professional graphic designer, it empowers me to efficiently create and disseminate posts to my target audience. On numerous occasions, I have utilized the *Canva* mobile app to produce engaging social media posts, swiftly uploading them to various platforms. *Canva* proves exceptionally useful when I need to swiftly create lead magnets to attract potential customers. Whether it's crafting visually appealing graphics for social media post or designing eye-catching graphics for blog post, *Canva* consistently proves to be a valuable asset, allowing me to optimize both time and financial resources.

> **"While (Canva) doesn't replace the expertise of a professional graphic designer, it empowers me to efficiently create and disseminate posts to my target audience.**

Why you should consider adding this technology platform to help you launch, grow, or scale your business

I know that as female business owners, a lot of times we don't have the confidence that we need in either the products or the services that we offer. With *Canva*, you can launch, scale, and grow your business easily with a little bit of practice. You can start cranking out sales promotions, make social media posts, and create lead magnets. Launching your products and services can be easier and faster using Canva. You can add your brand colors to Canva to create logos, product graphics, and product mockup to use in the launch. You can use these graphics to test offers and get feedback from your audience without spending lots of money on graphics. It allows you to pivot quickly and inexpensively, while still being able to serve your customers.

Challenges I can help you avoid

A lot of times, because sales just seems so daunting, and so many people are afraid of sales, they feel like they don't know what to say or do when it comes to the sales process, or they didn't even know that there was a sales process. So, we help them to have a mindset shift. Believe it or not, most sales start in your mind. We help our clients to get unstuck when it comes to the sales and selling process. There are several ways through which we sell.

> **"Believe it or not, most sales start in your mind. We help our clients to get unstuck when it comes to the sales and selling process.**

We can show them how to reach their audience and how to leave them feeling competent in the process. We also allow them to figure out a sales process or a sales technique that works best for them and show them that sales is a teachable skill, and it does not have to be intimidating. We allow them to be able to be confident in their own skills and competent in their product, knowing that there is a need for their product and that everyone needs to hear about it.

How you can go further faster

I coach, mentor, and train entrepreneurs and sales professionals on how to increase their sales. Now, we do live in a DIY society; that's why we not only offer one-on-one coaching, but we also offer online courses and group coaching. What this does is, it allows everyone to be able to work at their own pace and also allows them to achieve their goals. A lot of times we might not be ready to do one-on-one coaching. Some women might feel more comfortable working online because they haven't gained the confidence needed in order to help them in their sales process. Again, that's why we offer online and in-person coaching.

The benefits of leveraging this technology

There are so many challenges when promoting your products and services, that it's crucial to differentiate yourself from the competition. One effective way to achieve this is by harnessing the power of graphics. Many individuals prefer visual content over reading lengthy texts, as they say, "a picture is worth a thousand words." By utilizing graphics, whether it be through pictures, captions, or showcasing end results, you can effectively capture people's attention. *Canva* provides you with the opportunity to create graphics quickly and easily from your desktop or your phone. This convenience empowers you to produce visually appealing content without the need for extensive design skills or sophisticated equipment. By using *Canva*, you can create compelling graphics that will help your brand stand out and also engage your target audience.

A successful outcome

One of my favorite clients is one of our agents. She had been following our social media posts and noticed the content I shared on Facebook and Instagram. After watching our social media for months, one day she called me and said "Will you mentor me? Will you be my coach?" and I said "I definitely will." She said that she wanted to be able to promote herself and her business in a professional manner. I introduced her to *Canva*, and guided her through its features. Together, we created a few designs, and I demonstrated how to navigate the platform effectively.

> **One of my favorite clients told me, "I love your social media posts." "Will you mentor me? Will you be my coach?" And I said, "I definitely will."**

Since I had a collection of graphics I had made for the agency, I shared them with her. She was able to customize and personalize these graphics to suit her business needs. I was impressed by her quick grasp of the platform's capabilities.

Word spread among the other agents. I had a number of agents asking me to show them how to create quality graphics for their agencies. During a training session I conducted, I taught them all how to use *Canva* effectively. After the training, I shared numerous graphics that I had created with the agents. This became a game changer in the agency not only for us but also for the agents who were able to promote themselves and their business with graphics

Things were challenging for me, too, until I leveraged this technology

Being a woman entrepreneur, I understand the struggles associated with content creation. It seemed like everyone was emphasizing the importance of creating content for my business and audience. "Content is king," they would say. However, I found myself unsure about what type of content to produce and what would resonate with my audience and customers.

I took a step back and conducted thorough research. That's when I realized that visuals and graphics have a strong allure for many people. *Canva* became my go-to tool, enabling me to present information in easily digestible and visually appealing formats. With *Canva,* I could provide my audience with bite-sized pieces of information that they could easily consume and take action on.

A lesson I learned

I have learned is that it's okay to feel uncomfortable, although it was initially challenging for me to accept. We assume that feeling uncomfortable is inherently negative, but in reality, it can foster tremendous growth. Embracing discomfort allowed me to expand as an entrepreneur and as an individual. During the early stages of my entrepreneurial endeavors I didn't know what to say, or what I should be doing. I was uncomfortable, this motivated me to take classes, read books, attend seminars, and experiment with different technology. Me being uncomfortable made me grow!

Questions you should ask yourself . . .

One of the most important things to reflect upon is your personal dreams and aspirations. As a woman, it's crucial to ask yourself the following questions:

1.   **What have I always dreamed about doing?** Take some time to identify and acknowledge your deepest aspirations. What activities or achievements have always captured your imagination and ignited your passion?

2. What obstacles are hindering me from pursuing my dreams? It's common for women to prioritize their family or put their dreams on hold indefinitely. Explore the factors that have held you back from pursuing your aspirations, whether they are external circumstances or internal barriers.

3. What steps can I take to transform my dreams into reality? Once you've identified your dreams and acknowledged the obstacles, it's time to develop an action plan. Break down your dreams into smaller, manageable goals and determine the practical steps needed to accomplish them.

Remember, dreams do not have an expiration date. It is within your power to make them come true. By dedicating time to sit down, set goals, and outline the necessary steps, you can actively pursue and achieve your aspirations. Embrace the belief that you can accomplish any dream you set your mind to.

My recommendation

My recommendation regarding the utilization of technology is to overcome the fear associated with it and embrace its potential. Often, we tend to focus solely on the technical aspects, which can be intimidating. However, it is important to recognize that technology can be advantageous to us. Instead of fearing it, take the time to familiarize yourself with it and learn how to utilize it effectively. Not all tools will be suitable for your specific needs, but when you discover those that work well, make the most of them in your business. Utilize them to their fullest extent and leverage their capabilities to enhance your operations. Once again, the key is to eliminate the fear surrounding technology and be willing to explore different options to determine what works best for you.

Connect with me. I can help you!

Renee Coakley can be found on www.theclosingacademy.com. Please follow like and share @theclosingacademy on Facebook, Twitter, Linkedin, Instgram, Youtube and on all social media platforms.   You can go to Canva.com and sign up for an account. You can also download the app to your phone. Let me know how you are using Canva in your business.

Download our FREE Guide, "Top Ten Selling Secrets For People That HATE To SELL," at www.theclosingacademy.com.

A bit about me and the difference I can make working with you

The name of my company is *The Closing Academy*. We teach entrepreneurs and sales professionals how to sell. We believe that sales is a teachable skill.

The idea of selling makes most people uncomfortable. It's natural for most people to have some fear. No matter what business you're in, **you need to learn sales skills.** There are people out there who are waiting to hear about your products and services, but a lot of times, people are too afraid to ask for the sale, or they're not sure how to ask for the sale. So, what we do is, we teach entrepreneurs that sales can be as easy as a conversation.

I teach people how to sell, how to have a positive mindset, and allow them to develop the competence that they need in order to make the sale. These changes can help them grow from a five-figure to a six-figure company. We've helped agents go from making a few thousand in sales to making hundreds of thousands in sales. So, by working with us and by learning the techniques that we teach, you will also increase your sales.

> **"I teach people how to sell, how to have a positive mindset, and allow them to develop the competence that they need.**

A lot of times, when people think of sales, they think of the hard sell. They don't think about adapting the sale to their personality or their technique. There are some people who are informational sellers; what they do is, they give information so that you can determine what you want to purchase and how you're able to purchase it.

My ideal client is an entrepreneur who is new to sales and is eager to develop the necessary skills to become a successful salesperson. Often, I encounter new business owners who express enthusiasm about their wonderful product and its ability to solve various problems. However, they hesitate to promote their products and fear asking for the sale.

While they enthusiastically describe the product's benefits, they struggle to follow through by asking questions like, "How many would you like?" or "How can I process your order?" At our company, we work with these entrepreneurs to help them gain confidence and realize that sales is no longer intimidating. It's important to understand that we sell ourselves every day through our appearance and the smiles we wear on our faces. Our goal is to make sales a natural and integral part of everyday business.

What makes me different is, that I am the cofounder of an award-winning insurance agency, *Coakley Financial Group*. I work side by side with my husband, Calbert Coakley, and together, we have helped agents reach and exceed their sales goal. We know what works because we've taught our agents these skills. A lot of people are struggling, trying to figure out, "Does this work?" or "Does this not work?"

We know that our sales processes and our sales techniques work because we've used them with our agents. These skills have been key to their success in the sales arena and to the success of our agency, and because of this success, we've been sought out to develop and train other sales professionals. We have done sales trainings both online or in person. We've had people come to us and ask for help with closing the sales on their webinars.

What makes *The Closing Academy* different is that we're not working out a theory. We have put these techniques into practice, so we know that it works, and we know that there are proven sales skills that you and everyone can learn.

The problems my company helps solve

We teach entrepreneurs and sales professionals how to sell, and we help clients increase their sales. We assist them in creating tactics and strategies to increase their sales. The company was started out of a need, as there were agents from other agencies coming to us and asking us for training. They were asking us what we were doing in training sessions, and then we quickly realized that there was a need for sales training.

We also realized that there were a lot of people out there who were afraid of sales. So, one of the things that we did was to offer training sessions that

> **"We teach entrepreneurs and sales professionals how to sell, and we help clients increase their sales.**

included training other agents. A lot of times, most of our agents ended up being the top agents in Georgia or within their career. *The Closing Academy* came about out of a need to coach and mentor. We have been in business for over 10 years.

Our agency is a culmination of us working within the agency, finding out what worked and what didn't work, being able to have our agents implement the techniques and then teaching others how to implement those same sales techniques.

How I overcame a challenging stage in my business

Overcoming a challenging stage in our business required addressing the initial hurdle of effectively promoting our services. Although we were known within our community and people were aware of the services we offered, we recognized the need to reach a broader audience. Our expertise lies in teaching and training business owners in the art of selling, and we understood that our services held immense value for a larger audience. It was disheartening to see entrepreneur's express excitement about their products but struggle with the fear of selling.

To overcome this obstacle, we realized the importance of spreading the word about how we could help solve this need. We embarked on a thorough and thoughtful process of determining the best approach to reach our potential customers. Utilizing graphic visuals, we developed materials that explained our unique process and showcased the benefits of our products. This visual representation helped convey our message in a compelling way, capturing the attention of our target audience.

What did you learn from this chapter or this book? Feel free to use the #SheThinksLikeACEO hashtag and let us know. On the two pages following this chapter, you'll be able to record your thoughts and Aha's.

Renee Coakley is an accomplished sales and marketing expert operating a six-figure business that continues to earn profit. She teaches entrepreneurs and sales professionals how to improve sales by leveraging the power of good graphic design in their marketing strategy, increasing visibility and brand awareness.

Website:	www.theclosingacademy.com
Location:	Atlanta, Georgia
Facebook:	www.facebook.com/theclosingacademy
Twitter:	www.twitter.com/reneecoakley
	www.twitter.com/ClosingAcademy
LinkedIN:	www.linkedin.com/in/reneecoakley
LinkedIN:	www.linkedin.com/company/the-closing-academy/

Use this area to journal your thoughts
surrounding your Aha's from this chapter.

Use this area to journal your thoughts
surrounding your Aha's from this chapter.

"Effective partnership enables more potent success than can be accomplished alone."

~Selena P. Teems

Get Targeted Leads Without Having To Pay For Them

Don't have a budget to hire expensive marketing firms to help you get leads?

As of January 2023, Facebook had 2.963 billion monthly active users, and Facebook Groups had 1.8 billion users. As of August 2022, there were over 10 million Facebook Groups.

If you can think of a topic, **there's a Facebook Group for it.** Facebook Groups are virtual places where people with common interests share concepts, ideas, and opinions, upload photos, post valuable content, engage in chat rooms, live streams and most importantly post their pain points in comments. Facebook Groups are a goldmine for business owners looking to make business connections.

Do you struggle to get a regular flow of leads?

Do you lack a budget to purchase paid advertising?

You can accomplish two things at one time by joining Facebook Groups:

1)   You can establish yourself as an authority or thought leader, and

2)   You can make new connections.

To start attracting leads, you must first become visible and add value to the group. If you join a group with the sole purpose of getting leads, you will be removed from the group.

Selena P. Teems is a native of New Orleans, LA., graduate of an HBCU, Florida Memorial University, and proud mother of two remarkable young men. She created the *Indie Author Market*™, a self-publishing marketplace to serve authors and freelancers. The platform solves problems for independent authors, and she leveraged Facebook Groups to find her ideal prospects.

Sit back and learn about a technology that can make a difference in your business. Selena will share how she leveraged Facebook Groups to find prospects and how she can help you also launch, grow, or scale your business and achieve a greater level of success!

A Conversation with Selena P. Teems

The technology platform that made a difference in my business is *Facebook, specifically Facebook Groups.* By joining and communicating in Facebook groups, I was able to connect with thousands of writers and authors by virtually hanging out. This allowed them to openly express their frustrations and goals. By working in self-publishing, I was able to expand my thought process and explore possible solutions for them. What I learned in Facebook groups made the difference in how I created *Indie Author Market*™. The *Indie Author Market*™ is designed to solve problems identified by independent authors and the freelance publishing community. Before I created the *Indie Author Market*™, I felt like there were more connections needed than I could make between authors and freelancers. It was frustrating not being able to offer author clients the specific professionals to support them in reaching their target audience.

What was hard before I leveraged this technology

There are highly recommended freelancers who, due to their workload, are often not able to serve more clients. This can have a negative impact on an author's publishing timeline, prelaunch, and marketing campaigns. That was a point of frustration and the impetus for creating a solution to address these two issues.

What changed for me implementing this technology

By creating the Indie Author Market™, the issue of imbalance in matching authors to specific freelancers and the lack of availability of freelancers was also solved. We can host a large pool of freelance professionals for indie authors. The self-publishing marketplace brings all the publishing parties into the same virtual room to create high quality, literary work. Also, another change with the *Indie Author Market*™ is the ability to stimulate business activity through discounted unique offers on the platform. Featured deals are a part of the platform, as well as subscription packages. There are a wide variety of offerings that can be developed in order to meet the needs of indie authors. I could only facilitate connections with freelancers I knew or that I had personally researched. This marketplace allows rich talent to come to the platform, be vetted as a verified business, and then offer those services to independent authors.

> **"The Indie Author Market™ has the ability to stimulate business activity through discounted, unique offers on the platform.**

How I overcame a challenging stage in my business

I struggled with "Imposter Syndrome." I worried that I was not qualified to advise authors on self-publishing. I overcame that fear by going above and beyond to ensure that the information I provided to clients was accurate and useful for moving them forward to completing the publishing process. I accepted the fact that I could not be right 100% all of the time, but I was sufficient and thorough in making every effort to provide the best information available to my clients.

Why it is important to have a coach, consultant, or mentor

Every female entrepreneur, especially a female-owned business, should work with a coach, hire a consultant, or have a mentor because business mistakes can be costly. The second reason to have a coach, consultant, or mentor is that as a business owner, we are often very focused on operations, and there are peripheral matters that need consideration for us in order to have balance in our business. A coach, consultant, or mentor is someone who can objectively bring those peripheral issues to your attention. The third reason is that either of the professionals I mentioned could serve as part of your support system in business. They are your sounding board, a source of encouragement to keep moving forward when business challenges become overwhelming. I have a business coach.

How this technology will make a difference in your business

With many female-owned businesses being a one-woman operation, along with staying relevant requires embracing technology—in particular, technology that makes your life and business easier. On the Indie Author Market platform, you can perform numerous business management tasks through a front-end dashboard that includes a booking calendar, internal messaging with clients, product advertisement, and much more. You would be able to create spontaneous front-end offers to clients on the platform, thereby increasing the opportunity for revenue generation.

> "A member would be able to create spontaneous front-end offers to clients on the platform, thereby increasing the opportunity for revenue generation.

Why you should consider adding this technology platform to help you launch, grow, or scale your business

Any platform that allows a one-woman business to execute multiple key business functions, in one place, is a definite must-have. This technology can be leveraged to "buy back" hours that can be dedicated to enjoying life such as family, community, etc.

Challenges I can help you avoid

Successful YOU!® helps clients publish books successfully and can help you avoid the critical mistake of publishing poor quality work. We can help you avoid the expense and frustration of delays in publishing because of the types of engagements that are available on the platform. We have built-in accountability systems that would take into consideration the author's scheduled book launch date.

How you can go further faster

It is advantageous for female CEOs, entrepreneurs, and business owners in the publishing industry to work with Successful YOU!®.

We've solved the most frustrating aspects of the self-publishing process for authors and created a way to incentivize excellence in publishing.

Everyone has gifts, abilities, and natural talents, yet you really aren't experts in all things. The smart money business philosophy says to double- and triple-down on your strengths and add team members that are talented in your areas of weakness. I agree with this philosophy, particularly for businesses in the scale and growth stages. It is inefficient and quite expensive to try to be something that you are not. My book, *The Power of Diligence,* states that if specialized knowledge is needed, determine whether it is more important for you to become a specialist or to seek aid.

The benefits of leveraging this technology

Leveraging the Successful YOU!® Indie Author Market platform, as well as Facebook groups, will alleviate the need for a female entrepreneur, CEO, or business owner to search multiple platforms for the publishing talent that she requires. The benefits are that she can engage with self-publishing professionals, and she could save time and money by "one-stop shopping" her publishing needs.

A successful outcome

Shortly after opening Successful YOU!®, I worked with a wonderful woman author. She had a completed manuscript and needed help getting it published. We reviewed self-publishing versus traditional publishing models and the milestones for each process. She decided to self-publish and is successfully marketing that book while she works on her second book. This client could now look forward to a simplified process and specific freelance professionals to work with in order to complete her book.

Things were challenging for me, too, until I leveraged this technology

> **"As a female business owner, I used to struggle with disappointment when good faith transactions went awry.**

As a female business owner, I used to struggle with disappointment when good faith transactions went awry. I would take too much time to rebound and to move forward with the next transaction. I would have a *Plan B* and a *Plan C,* but I would often feel decidedly vested in *Plan A.* Thats' no longer a challenge because I'm very busy and do not have the luxury of ruminating over one step in the master plan. I would offer that same advice to any other woman in business that is starting out.

Time is precious, and so, when something does not work out according to plan, the ability to reassess and move forward is the ultimate key in the consistency and growth of your business. So, hopefully, it would be an early challenge and not something that plagues a business well into its operational years.

A lesson I learned

A lesson I learned early on as an entrepreneur that changed the way I do business today is to not defer to the expertise of others when it doesn't feel right in my gut.

> **❝A lesson I learned early on as an entrepreneur that changed the way I do business today is to not defer to the expertise of others when it doesn't feel right in my gut.**

An example of a mistake I made is with my business website. I hired a digital marketing consultant to reach sales targets. As part of the package of services, I received a very impressive website theme. It had many features that my business had not yet expanded to use but I could grow into it. After a successful engagement with the consultant, I began to work with someone new to customize the features of the site. My gut said keep what I have and grow into it, but because I considered the new web designer more of an expert I went with his suggestion.

Needless to say, the delivered website was well short of what I had at first. After many frustrating interactions I was able to get the original theme re-installed. I learned to be clear in my expectations, to communicate more effectively and to respect my intuition in business.

Questions you should ask yourself

The most important type of question a woman should ask when considering her desired future position, is one that empowers possibility thinking. Ask "how can I" questions. Ask, "What would it take for me to ...?" Fill in the blanks with your business goals. Avoid disempowering questions such as "Why can't I ever ...?" The 'why' questions will give you reasons, and those reasons will be consistent with your general mindset.

If you feel down about your success, your mind will return negative reasons why. Depending on your emotional state and your default mindset, when you ask "why" questions, you're going to get responses that reinforce your personal story.

What I am doing continuously and encouraging women to do is rewrite that personal story. Move into a future that looks nothing like your present. That is why you are in business and why you are pursuing excellence. I strongly encourage women to ask questions that open possibilities and solutions and avoid questions that keep you stuck in your current story.

My recommendation

My recommendation to a woman reading this book or my chapter about using technology or using the Indie Author Market™ would be to ask, "How can I use technology to serve my customers?" Asking that question will lead you to a solution that will elevate your business, help you to grow, and certainly help you to serve more customers because technology enables us to do so.

Connect with me. I can help you!

To find out more about Indie Author Market, visit www.indieauthor. market. We are transforming indie publishing, the self-publishing market, one step at a time. Indie Author App, a mobile application is in the beta stage and we would love to have you as a beta tester. Please email us at info@sypublishnow.com or visit us on any of our platforms.

A bit about me and the difference I can make working with you

My company is Successful YOU!® We enable independent authors and freelancers to find each other, transact business, produce quality books through the Indie Author Market™ and our self-publishing marketplace. We connect authors with freelance talent, which includes but is not limited to: editors, illustrators, narrators, audiobook production, publishing rights, representation, book cover design, marketing and every aspect of the publishing process that an independent author would engage in order to publish a high-quality book.

One problem I specialize in solving is simplifying the commerce between independent authors and freelance

> **"Working with us you can achieve better quality, independent, early-published books; the other is small business growth in the publishing sector.**

publishing professionals on the Indie Author Market™ platform. An author would be able to view and review a variety of freelance professionals, engage in a dialogue regarding their services, request a quote—which can be accepted or rejected—and then proceed to a transaction. The author pays for the services, and the freelancer commences the work for the author. We simplify the process on one platform for authors to hire the professional talent needed to publish their books.

There are two outcomes that can be achieved by working with Successful YOU!® One is better quality, independent, easily-published books; the other is small business growth in the publishing sector. This means that we are promoting and stimulating activity among solopreneurs that provide freelance services.

By helping a female entrepreneur maximize the audience for her creative content, we can increase the quality and distribution channels for her products and services.

The ideal client for Successful YOU!® is a content creator who is looking to publish impactful work and who makes personal and financial investments to accomplish her goal.

I am an independent author, so I speak from the perspective of having gone through the process. I bring my personal experiences to the platform. I am transforming self-publishing through technology, creating a clear path to independent publishing and promoting small business growth.

The problems my company helps solve

This all-in-one business model successfully solves the problem of a negative narrative around the quality of self-published literary content compared to traditionally published books. Successful YOU! ® provides affordable high-quality services in independent publishing.

Successful YOU!® also facilitates successful engagements between authors and freelance professionals by helping authors define their needs and goals for publishing. We match them with choices among a pool of qualified customer-service-focused publishing professionals to deliver on those needs. We have been connecting authors and publishing professionals since 2011.

What did you learn from this chapter or this book? Feel free to use the #SheThinksLikeACEO hashtag and let us know. On the two pages following this chapter, you'll be able to record your thoughts and Aha's.

Selena Teems is a native of New Orleans, LA., graduate of Florida Memorial University, a HBCU and proud mother of two remarkable young men. I founded Successful YOU!® in 2011 to solve problems for independent authors and with technology, created Indie Author Market™, an online self-publishing marketplace to serve authors and freelancers.

Website:	www.indieauthor.market
Email:	info@sypublishnow.com
Location:	Miami, Florida
Facebook:	www.facebook.com/SYPUBLISHNOW
Instagram:	indie_author_market
Twitter:	www.twitter.com/SYpublishnow
LinkedIN:	www.linkedin.com/in/sypublishnow

Use this area to journal your thoughts surrounding your Aha's from this chapter.

Use this area to journal your thoughts
surrounding your Aha's from this chapter.

"Everyone deserves to be the best version of themselves."

~Stacy London

Using Media to Build Confidence and Solve Branding & Visibility Challenges

Are you struggling to stand out?

With so much noise in almost every industry, and each business vying for the same customer's attention, how are you positioning yourself to stand out from all the others?

Have you considered creating an audio & video Podcast?

According to demandsage.com **41%** of people in the US tune into podcasts **at least once a month**, and *Morning Consult* found that nearly (32%) of Americans said they prefer listening to **podcasts with video.**

Podcasts and videos have become a way to stand out in the marketplace. The great thing about it is you don't need someone's approval to start your own. I remember thinking, "Who am I to start a Podcast?" "Who's going to listen to me or what I have to say in a podcast?"

At first, I believed you had to have a certain level of experience before creating one. However, I learned otherwise.

If you enjoy listening to podcasts, what is it about the world of podcasting that has you hooked?

If you think that your ideal audience won't be interested in what you have to share on your podcast, you are mistaken. Your audience craves listening to you the same way you listen to someone else.

Creating a web show is another opportunity to craft amazing video content that positions you as the expert, a thought leader, and allows you to control the narrative of your brand.

If you're thinking, "Well everyone is already doing it, why should I jump into that crowded arena?" you'll miss out on real opportunities.

Here's a reality check, out of a population of **almost 8 billion people,** there are **only 2 million podcasts** worldwide, according to Oberlo.com. Those numbers include company podcasts, celebrity podcasts, along with podcasters who have multiple shows. There's still a blue ocean of opportunity out there for **your** message.

> **"Out of a population of almost 8 billion people, there are only 2million podcasts worldwide**

Oberlo shares that 3 out of 4 podcast listeners tune in to learn something new. So if your message is geared towards educating others, **BAM** - you have a winner. If you do this right, it can also be another stream of income for you through advertising because more than half of listeners buy based on an ad they heard during a podcast. **Cha Ching!**

Alicia Couri is the CEO of **Audacious Concepts Inc.,** a boutique consulting firm that specializes in helping leaders and their teams work better together. She's the founder of **RedCarpetCEO**™ a digital media & personal branding company with a successful podcast and several online web shows. She has earned numerous accolades for her exceptional work, including the prestigious *G9-Global Icon Award* at the *First Ladies Forum* in Dubai. Alicia was named the Top *Audacious Confidence Growth Expert* by the International Association of Top Professionals for 2022 and a recipient of *the Empowered Woman Award for 2023*, Alicia is a multi-award-winning international TEDx speaker, author, and *Legacy Queen for Woman of Achievement*. Alicia has appeared on ABC, CBS, NBC, and multiple radio shows and podcasts.

Sit back and quickly learn about a technology that can make a difference in your business. Alicia Couri will share how leveraging Podcasts can help you launch, grow, or scale and achieve a greater level of success!

A Conversation with Alicia Couri

The technology platform that I leveraged

Podcasts & Streaming Webshows on Television are the technology platforms I want to share with you.

I was introduced to *Podetize,* a total solution for podcasting a few years ago. A few years later, as *Win Win Women* TV launched, I created a show on that platform. *Win Win Women* is a global platform that hosts live webshows **for women by women** 24 hours a day. They then distribute the shows to a worldwide audience leveraging their website, *Roku, Amazon TV & Apple+*. These platforms have made it possible for women anywhere in the world to produce high quality content and **gain visibility & credibility.**

What was hard before I leveraged this technology

Years ago when I started live streaming on *Facebook* and *Youtube*, I got used to being on those platforms, but was so intimidated to create a podcast for myself even though people encouraged me to start one. At first I felt I didn't have what it took to do all the things necessary to launch a proper podcast because it required sound editing and uploading to the specific podcast platforms. Because I lived in the world of livestreaming videos, I didn't recognize the value and panache of having my own podcast. At the time I wanted to meet more decision makers in businesses and realized that the audience I was attracting with the webshows wasn't the audience I could do business with. I needed a way to get corporate decision makers as contacts. Back then, starting a podcast wasn't as accessible to create, distribute, **attract and grow** your audience as it is today. I paid for a course but never got past Module #1 lol. The learning curve was too much for me to get proficient and still build my new business.

What changed for me implementing this technology

After implementing the right approach with *Podetize & Win Win Women,* my influence grew. I was able to attract the right audience of leaders both entrepreneurs and corporate leaders. It has given me a very valuable and leverageable platform that attracts leaders globally who listen and especially want to be guests. As a matter of fact, every week I am bombarded by emails and Linkedin messages from people who want to be an expert guest on my podcast and our download numbers keep growing.

Additionally, my speaking busines has increased because of my visibility and consistency and I have been able to create an entirely new stream of income with advertisers. Because of my media presence, I was invited to become a part of the *Black Owned Media Alliance* and serve as their marketing chairperson.

> **"Partnerships can sometimes be a challenge especially when things go south. I used to run a done for you streaming production service with a partner, but when our ideas for how the business should run diverged and we couldn't agree on anything**

How I overcame a challenging stage in my business

Partnerships can sometimes be a challenge, especially when things go south. I used to run a done for you streaming production service with a partner. However, when our ideas for how the business should run diverged and we couldn't agree on anything from how we acquired and communicated with the guests, to client acquisition, to social media copy, things went from difficult to unbearable for us both. It became clear that the partnership was deteriorating, the business was suffering, and I had to find a way out. I left the business but was faced with either stopping my shows altogether, or figuring out how to do all of the processes myself. From guest acquisition to the actual production, all the video intros, graphics, social media promotions etc, etc.

I decided to persevere and to keep producing shows on my own. My assistant and I figured it all out and now we have a seamless process and team for filming, editing, production and promotion. Our graphics templates are strongly branded, we have copywriting templates, and now with the help of AI we're able to edit copy more efficiently. We have email templates, calendar templates with automatic links, and social post with stories. We are a well oiled machine, a far cry from how things were happening with the partnership.

Why it's important to have a coach, consultant, or mentor

As a business consultant and coach, I strongly believe in coaches and mentors. They are experts at seeing what you don't see and pulling out of you the necessary ingredients for your success. They can help you collapse the time it took them to learn and do it so you can achieve it faster, more effectively, and save you time, lots of money and many heartaches. Without my mentor at the time, I wouldn't have had the courage to do this on my own. But their belief in me helped me believe in myself.

How this technology will make a difference in your business

There are so many amazing benefits for women-owned businesses that utilize the technology platform of *Win Win Women TV.*

> **"There are so many amazing benefits for women owned businesses that utilizing the technology platform of Win Win Women TV will dramatically help a woman running a business.**

This platform will dramatically help a woman running a business. The best part of this platform is the ease of use. When you become a show host, Win Win Women provides everything for you including training, especially is you've never hosted a show before. With *Podetize,* they produce the entire podcast after you create the recording. Both audio and video production is included in their service, saving you time, money and frustration because you don't have to touch anything after recording.

But why should you even consider becoming a show host or launch a podcast?

There are so many benefits:
1. It will **increase** your visibility reach to your ideal audience
2. It will put you **in front of more people** to expand your network
3. If you have a brand, this will solidify you as a thought leader
4. As the voice of your own show, you will **become an inspiration to others and create fans**
5. **Increase** your clientele
6. You'll have an opportunity to **raise your prices**

Why you should consider adding this technology platform to help you launch, grow, or scale your business

You may have been told that you have to do *Instagram Live*, you have to do *Facebook Live*, you have post on *X* (formerly Twitter), you have to do *YouTube Live*, you have to do *Snapchat*, you have to do *LinkedIn*, and you have to do all of that, plus run your business.

However, there are a few challenges: The learning curve for all those social media platforms is extremely time consuming. It takes time to develop how to do it right and to gather an audience on each platform. Oh, the marketing struggles! How do you market on each of those platforms? Do you have the proper graphics, content, and copyrighting support? Consider the confusion of all the different tools out there. There are so many. Podcasting is one piece of content that you can utilize in many ways on each platform.

> **"They just said that I needed to do live video to grow my audience and my business, but what did that really mean?**

Challenges I can help you avoid

I was told over and over by coaches that I needed to be on video. They just said that I needed to do live video to grow my audience and my business, but what did that really mean?

I thought I would just turn on the camera and do the video, and boom, the audience would magically show up. Well, that doesn't happen. I did videos every day for months, and I uploaded a lot onto YouTube, but guess what?

Without the right platform, without the right strategy, my videos did not get traction, and I see this so often on Facebook and YouTube where people are throwing out content, throwing up videos, and you see their videos only have like five views and no likes. There's so much out there to do videos on, but without the right strategy, no one notices.

I can help you create the right strategy for your show/podcast and align it with your brand. My team can get you the visibility your podcast or webshow needs.

How you can go further faster

I have been a solopreneur for a long time, and I am big on DIY, but it has hindered my business. It has slowed me down and kept me from getting where I needed to be. I'm a wife, a mother of three, a volunteer, and I have several businesses that I run, and I constantly struggle to give my all to everything and everyone. Something must suffer, and a lot of times, I was the one who suffered.

If you truly want to develop a strong brand for your business and have a unique voice in the marketplace that stands out and gets you noticed as the authority in your industry, you need strong video and audio content. These services can help you step out powerfully.

> **"If you truly want to develop a strong brand for your business and have a unique voice in the marketplace that stands out and gets you noticed as the authority in your industry.**

But you cannot do this all on your own, especially if you are already running a business; it's exhausting. Having a service that will do it all for you, from editing your content, repurposing it, creating the right graphics, etc. There's a lot to do in order to elevate yourself to the level of elite business owners, and I'm telling you, you cannot continue to be the "Jack of all trades" in your business and also gain tremendous success.

The benefits of leveraging this technology

Do you have something to say? A point of view that's different than others that needs a voice? Leveraging Podcasts and Webshows is an opportunity to become a SME - Subject Matter Expert. The great thing about hosting podcasts is being invited to be on more and more podcasts as well which helps you spread your message even further.

With podcasting you can become the go-to person in your industry. But it will call for you to step out and let people know about you, and your brilliance.

A successful outcome

Transitioning your business is never easy. Rebranding from one established brand to something completely new and different comes with even more challenges than creating a brand from scratch.

I was transitioning from the beauty business to consulting, speaking, and coaching. I needed to have coaches and mentors of my own to help me get there. I took two bold steps in my rebrand.

1. I hired a coach and learned how to book myself on local television stations all over the country, and

2. I wrote a book that would help me get booked on TV. Being on TV opened up doors for greater opportunities for me. That step led

me to being more comfortable on camera, which got me noticed by an independent movie director/produer.

Having those opportunities grew my confidence exponentially and gave me the courage to launch my podcast "Leading with Audacious Confidence."

My motto is "I am here to influence, educate, inspire, and entertain you so you can step into your Audacious Confidence and be more, do more, have more, and live the life of your dreams without limits or restrictions" because I learned to walk that path.

Things were challenging for me too until I leveraged this technology

As a female business owner, I really struggled with my own confidence and ability to do it all. I struggled with my limiting beliefs, my many blind spots. As a mother of three, I've always put my family first. It was challenging for me to find the time or rather invest the time I needed in my business to get it to where I wanted it to be.

As I mentioned earlier, I had to overcome a lot of hurdles, especially when it came to visibility. But it was necessary in order to grow from where I was in order to market, promote, and brand myself. Having a rock solid brand will help you attract the right audience will take a lot of pressure off of you. It will also buy back a lot of your time to help you influence others and become the authority **in your marketplace.**

A lesson I learned

I learned a lot of lessons as an entrepreneur early on. First, I had to learn that as much as I loved hair and makeup, my passion had now become my job. I had absolutely no problems investing in my training and my education when it came to developing and honing my skills and my craft as a hair and makeup artist, but I completely neglected to invest in myself, my own growth as the CEO.

I continued to do the same things over and over that seemed like it would work, but alas they didn't. I heard somewhere, that's the definition of insanity—to do the same things over and over, expecting different results. It wasn't until I finally hired a mindset coach, took some assessments on myself and really learned about me that I finally learned to let go. Coaches and mentors were my saving grace. They saw my potential, they pushed me when I needed to be pushed and steered me in the right direction when I needed to be steered. I learned so much more about myself. What's more valuable, **I learned how to love and appreciate myself.**

Questions you should ask yourself . . .

I learned from one of my mindset coaches and mentors, David Neagle, that two of the best questions to ask yourself when you're looking at where you are and where you want to go are, "What do I want?" and "What am I resisting?" Then ask yourself, "Am I running away from something when I do this, or am I running toward something that I really want?"

If you can honestly answer those questions, then you will heighten your awareness of yourself and know where you are honestly. Then and only then can you create a realistic plan. This plan is based on how much you're really willing to do, what needs to get done to go where you want to go and get real results. If you are in resistance, and you're not consciously making yourself aware of your resistances, you'll never get to where you want to go, and you'll create an unrealistic plan for yourself to get there.

My recommendation

Whether you're just starting out in business or if you've been in business for a while, I recommend being a show host with *Win Win Women*. It is the fastest, most cost-effective way to get going and you won't have to build your audience from scratch. *Win Win Women* already has a loyal following. The investment as well is not out of reach and you can create the show in many different ways.

> **"Whether you're just starting out in business or if you have been in business for a while, I would recommend being a show host with Win Win Women.**

If you check out my website **https://redcarpetceotm.now.site/home,** you can click on the "Win Win Women" Logo and it will take you right to the page to create your own show. Let me know when you do, so I can support your new show.

Connect with me. I can help you!

To find out more about me and the products and services that I provide, you can go to **audaciousconceptsinc.com.** You can also find out more about me on social media and on my other website, **alicia360.com.** On that link, you can connect with me on every social media platform. You can learn about my books and my videos and connect with me on *YouTube, Facebook, Twitter, LinkedIn, Instagram.*

For any personal branding, services or to find out how to create your own show/podcast, check out **redcarpetceo.com.**

If you are interested in podcasting and not sure where to start, I can connect you to some valuable sources that can either coach you to creating it for yourself, or do it all for you and all you need is to record your episode.

A bit about me and the difference I can make working with you

Female entrepreneurs are on the rise, and there's a demand from audiences to hear from more and more successful women in business. Building your authority to a direct and interactive audience increases your opportunity to attract more clients with live-streamed content. If you are apprehensive about being on camera, need to uplevel your brand or just need a confidence boost as a speaker, that's where I come in. My services revolve around confidence building, speaker training, storytelling, and camera confidence. I can also help you create a strategy for the structure of your show/podcast and help create a marketing strategy to super charge your launch. I've consulted with many new show hosts to help them start strong and confidently.

The problems my company helps solve

If you lack confidence to start your show, need speaker training, or you're lacking visibility or a brand that needs refining, we can help. We're ready to help you create a strategy to launch a great show/podcast, become an awesome host, and create an audience of fans that become clients. Just ask.

What did you learn from this chapter or this book? Feel free to use the #SheThinksLikeACEO hashtag and let us know. On the two pages following this chapter, you'll be able to record your thoughts and Aha's.

Alicia Couri, the CEO of Audacious Concepts Inc. a boutique consulting firm specializing in optimizing leaders & the dynamics of their teams. She is the recipient of the G9-Global Icon Award at the First Ladies Forum in Dubai and named the Top Audacious Confidence Growth Expert by the International Association of Top Professionals for 2022 and the Empowered Woman Award for 2023. She's an international speaker, author, actor, webshow & podcast producer/host and Legacy Queen for Woman of Achievement.

Alicia is especially passionate about inspiring Women to **own their awesome** by upleveling their confidence to step out with boldness.

Alicia and her team use brain science and people data tools to provide audacious solutions to the nagging and persistent people issues companies face clogging their revenue pipeline, including solutions for hiring the right people, clearing conflict, building trust, improving tough communication challenges & up-leveling a leaders brand capital just to name a few.

Alicia is a valued Advisory Board Member for Keiser University, the Marketing Chair for the Black Owned Media Alliance (BOMA) & Faculty for BoldHaus an INC 5000 Co.

Website:	www.redcarpetceo.com
	www.audaciousconceptsinc.com
Email:	alicia@aliciacouri.com
Location:	Miami, Florida
Facebook:	www.facebook.com/alicia.couri
Twitter:	www.twitter.com/thealiciacouri
LinkedIN:	www.linkedin.com/in/thealiciacouri
Instagram:	www.instagram.com/thealiciacouri

Use this area to journal your thoughts
surrounding your Aha's from this chapter.

Use this area to journal your thoughts
surrounding your Aha's from this chapter.

"One important factor in business success is quickly communicating value. Nothing helps you demonstrate your value faster than a well crafted brand video."

~Dr. Lori A. Manns

Video Marketing: A "Must-Have" For Today's Entrepreneur

Have you heard the saying, "A picture is worth a thousand words"?

Imagine how much more a video can capture and express your message to help your business grow.

It's proven that using video generates 12 times more shares than text and images on social media platforms. Additionally, customers purchase products at an increased rate of 64% after watching video content.

However, have you found it difficult to manage your video marketing or perhaps Facebook live broadcasts? Ever wondered how to utilize video effectively to create a strong marketing presence so you can build an audience and generate more sales?

Video marketing has emerged as the leading marketing tool that all businesses must implement for success in the new millennium. Video marketing is poised to become one of your best sales outlets that can work for you 24/7, 365 days a year.

These days, it is important to tap into the power of video marketing because it's a proven method allowing you to reach more prospects, convert more clients, and also retain current clients. Video helps with client retention because content creation enables you to be viewed as an authority or an expert in your industry or niche. Your clients will get value from the video content you share if it covers topics that matter to them.

Dr. Lori A. Manns is an accomplished business coach as well as sales.and marketing expert who teaches purpose driven entrepreneurs who to run profitable businesses. She is member of the esteemed Forbes Coaches Council and regular contributor to Forbes.com. Lori has also been featured in Who's Who In Black Atlanta consecutively, from 2010 to 2021.

Sit back and learn how utilizing video technology can make a big difference in your business. Dr. Lori will share how implementing video technology as a marketing strategy can help you launch, grow, and/or elevate your business to the next level and achieve greater success.

Conversation with Dr. Lori A. Manns

The technology platform that I'm going to talk about is *video marketing.* This marketing platform has made a huge difference in my business and can help any woman entrepreneur make a big difference in her business. Video speeds up the *know, like, and trust* factor. It positions women entrepreneurs as an expert and authority in their niche or field and gives them a platform for sharing their knowledge and expertise that will make them the 'go-to' person in their industry.

Video technology helps entrepreneurs attract ideal clients in a way that gives them an advantage over their competition and an advantage over people who are not using video.

Early on in my business, I learned that video marketing was one of the fastest ways to connect with small business owners and entrepreneurs through social media. The biggest way that video marketing made a difference for me was lead generation.

The sheer volume of people using YouTube was very attractive to me because there are billions of people using YouTube to search for and watch videos on anything and everything. Quite simply, that is why I started using video marketing to grow my business.

What was hard before I leveraged this technology?

Before I started using video marketing to grow my business, I felt like I was on a desert island in a foreign place, and no one knew who I was, or what I did for a living. After a few years of being in business, people still associated me with the corporate job that I had long since left. I knew it was time for me to get out there in a way that makes people understand that I was in business, working for myself, and ready to take on new consulting clients. I needed to establish my brand as a business strategist and coach. I needed people to see me as a brand and authority in my field.

It was by trial and error that I learned making videos to attract my ideal clients was a good idea. As it turns out, according to a research study done by *Think With Google*, 6 out of 10 people prefer to watch online video platforms as opposed to live TV. I figured out that I didn't need a huge marketing budget, TV budget, or radio budget to advertise my business. All I needed to do was put up videos on YouTube and on my website and share them on social media to get found, seen, and heard by prospects and people in my target market.

What changed for me implementing this technology?

What changed for me when I started to utilize video marketing to grow my business was, I became known as an expert and an authority. I was seen as someone who could speak on topics intelligently and share my expertise in a way that people could relate to. I knew if I shared valuable and insightful content to help people in areas where I was a subject matter expert, my name would be remembered.

> **❝Once I became seen as an expert and an authority in a certain area, the game changed.**

Video marketing helped people see me as someone who could educate and influence an audience and empower an audience at the same time. Once I became seen as an expert and an authority in a certain area, the game changed. I began getting invitations to speak on stages, radio shows, podcasts, and much more. Video changed the game for me because I started attracting people from all over the country, in the United States and the world. I began attracting people from countries like the UK, Australia, and even Russia. I began creating content where I was showcasing my expertise, and people noticed.

How I overcame a challenging stage in my business

During the launch phase of my business, I struggled with brand obscurity. It was also a struggle to get the type of clients that I wanted to work with. I overcame this challenge by figuring out who I really wanted to target. I learned how to create a message that would resonate with them. Once I created the right messaging, I had to figure out the best marketing vehicle to utilize to get my message across. I figured out the best marketing vehicle was video marketing. I used video marketing for lead generation and to get myself out there in a bigger way. Prospects would see me on video and feel like they already knew me. It was like instant fame. Just by virtue of what I was sharing, many prospects and clients could grasp that I knew what I was talking about.

Why it's important to have a coach, consultant, or mentor

There are three pivotal reasons why any entrepreneur should work with a coach. The number one reason would be that it saves you time. If you are weak in a certain area, a coach should be able to work with you to correct the weakest link. Another reason why entrepreneurs should hire a coach is to help them make money. A good business coach is going to show you strategies and tactics that are going to result in you producing more income. A good coach is going to show you how you can fast-track your income and make money faster, rather than if you were doing it all on your own. Without expert coaching and advice to shorten the learning curve, many entrepreneurs struggle to achieve their revenue goals. Another reason why you want to hire a coach is that it speeds up your success rate. I didn't hire a coach until I was in business a couple of years, and that created some issues for me because I could have increased my income a lot faster had I hired a coach sooner.

> **"There are three pivotal reasons why any entrepreneur should work with a coach. The number one reason would be that it saves you time.**

How this technology will make a difference in your business

Utilizing video marketing is a powerful way to reach your target market without breaking the bank. Leveraging video marketing is a great strategy to promote your brand and grow your business online.

According to *Small Biz Trends*, social video generates 12 times more shares than text and images on social media platforms. After watching a video, over 64% of users are more likely to buy a product online.

According to *HubSpot.com* and *RenderForest.com*, 53% of consumers engage with a brand after viewing a video on social media. All these statistics and facts prove that videos are a great way of increasing brand visibility and exposure as well as driving prospects to visit your website. Finally, video is a great way to get new followers on social media.

Why you should consider adding this technology platform to help you launch, grow, or scale your business

In my opinion, leveraging video marketing will help you to become an authority figure, a subject matter expert, and it will help you alleviate the problem of being an obscure brand. Video technology shortens the process of prospects getting to know you.

As a business owner, I struggled with being a big brand secret. I was the best-kept secret in my industry, niche, and city. However, once I started doing videos, I went from being a best-kept secret to being known as a business coach, sales coach, and an expert in my industry. I recommend women business owners use video marketing because it will catapult your success faster than any other marketing strategy out there.

If you don't like to be on camera, you can do explainer videos where you use your computer to talk about a subject and are using your voice to explain the topic. This way, you are using video to demonstrate your knowledge. Explainer videos are a great way to not only brand your company and your business but also promote your expertise without putting your face on camera.

> **"AI video generators automate video creation and editing without compromising on quality and allow you to make videos with just a few clicks.**

Another option is to utilize artificial intelligence video generators, which are next level. AI video generators automate video creation and editing without compromising on quality and allow you to make videos with just a few clicks. There are a few text to video tools that can assist you in making videos such as *GliaCloud*, *Synthesia*, and *InVideo* to name a few.

Most entrepreneurs agree that having videoss on your website and social media pages increases traffic, engagement, and conversions.

However, many people shy away from videos because they lack the expertise to create them. Now, you can use AI video creation tools to help you generate videos in no time flat.

Challenges I can help you avoid

The types of challenges I help my clients to avoid, number one, is being an unknown brand or business entity. When you are an unknown brand, or business, you don't get leads or clients, and your income is inconsistent. How can we help you get clients? By creating a marketing plan and a solid and profitable business strategy to put you in front of the right people. Exposure with the right audience is priceless.

Another challenge that we can help you with is inconsistent sales. We can help you level out your sales numbers by giving you a sales plan that will attract new ideal customers. We can help you level out your sales numbers by giving you a sales plan that will attract new ideal customers as well as retain existing ones.

How you can go further faster

It is advantageous for female CEOs to work with someone like me, even if they're in the growth or the scale stage, because I focus on developing your sales and business growth in a comprehensive, sustainable and scalable manner.

Many times, a business owner cannot see the big picture. If you're the frame, you can't see the picture. For this reason, you must have someone who is outside of your business and is capable of analyzing your business challenges in a comprehensive manner. With this approach, I am able to make recommendations that are aligned with the client's goals and make suggestions about steps they must take to win. A good business coach should be able to provide insight, resources, tools, suggestions, and advice on how to get to that next level and sustain it.

The benefits of leveraging this technology

In my opinion, leveraging video marketing will help you become an authority figure and a subject matter expert. Additionally, video helps to alleviate the problem of being an obscure brand.

A successful outcome

At one point, I had a realtor who was looking to grow her business by creating more opportunities for higher-priced listings and higher-priced home sales. I put together a marketing plan for this realtor who was not a fan of doing any digital marketing whatsoever. The marketing plan that I wrote included video marketing to attract the target market and position the realtor as the 'go-to' expert in the luxury real estate market in Atlanta.

In this plan, I created the content for her, the content calendar, and gave my client ideas about what to share, how to create the call to action, and when to post the videos. We also combined videos with live streaming on social media. People began watching my client's videos and started to share them, and before you knew it, the realtor began getting referrals. The best part was that someone referred my client to a potential client, and that ended up being a **million-dollar listing.**

However, I was not getting leads on a regular basis. I started doing videos, and I challenged myself to post them online consistently.

Things were challenging for me, too, in my business until I leveraged this technology

As a female business owner, I struggled with being an unknown brand and an unknown expert. I knew I was an expert in the areas of marketing, advertising, media, and sales because I had spent over 25 years in the industry. However, I was not getting leads on a consistent basis. I started doing videos, and I challenged myself to post them on consistently. Now, I'm a well-known speaker, influencer, subject matter expert, and authority figure in my niche because of video marketing. My video marketing strategy has gotten me invitations on blog posts, podcasts, radio shows, TV shows, you name it. I've been featured on Forbes.com, on Atlanta radio shows, and radio shows in other markets as well. I went from being an obscure unknown brand to being *a brand in demand.* Now I am regarded as a subject matter expert and being called upon for opportunities to speak on stages and on-air to share my knowledge and expertise.

> **"As a female business owner, I struggled with being an unknown brand and an unknown expert. I had spent over 25 years in the industry. However, I was not getting leads on a consistent basis.**

A lesson I learned

One lesson I learned early on in my business was that I had to stop doing everything myself. I had to **stop** being scared to hire a coach. I had to **stop being scared** to hire a virtual assistant or graphic designer or whatever I needed at the time. I had to **stop trying** to be superwoman and doing everything myself. I was burning the midnight oil, and I was burning myself out. If you don't want to spend money to invest in yourself, you are shooting yourself in the foot, and you probably won't have a successful business.

Early on, I had to learn that I couldn't rush the process of entrepreneurship. Entrepreneurship is **a journey, not a sprint.** I stopped trying to speed things up and learned to take each lesson day by day. I realized that the best approach in entrepreneurship is to learn as much as possible from each stage or phase as you go.

Questions you should ask yourself . . .

The most important question women should ask themselves in business is, "What is the number one thing I want to accomplish and why?" When you think about your long-term goals and the number one objective that you want to accomplish, it helps to put things in perspective.

Only then can you put together a plan to achieve that goal.

Every year, you should have a big audacious goal, and every month you should have smaller goals. Then you must ask yourself, Why do I want to accomplish this big goal? Once you've created monthly, quarterly, and yearly goals, you have something to reach for.

When women ask themselves this important question, "What's the number one thing I want to accomplish and why?" the answer helps them to achieve focus, clarity, and aids in establishing the vision for where they ultimately want to be.

> "The most important question women should ask themselves in business is, "What is the number one thing I want to accomplish and why?"

My recommendation

My recommendation for a woman reading this chapter about using video technology is to get comfortable using video because there are far more benefits and advantages than disadvantages. If you want to use video marketing in your business, you should create a strategy around it. The first step would be to create a goal for what you want video marketing to help you achieve in your business.

Secondly, reverse-engineer your goal by working backward. For example, if you want more clients, you must begin by identifying a need or a problem that you can help people solve. Only then can you begin to create video content that will attract those people who have the problem or challenge that your video addresses.

Thirdly, create a content calendar for topics that your ideal clients would be interested in and care about. Identify what topics you want to cover and tackle, one subject or one topic per month, and then delve into different subcategories of that topic. Once you do that, it's going to help you to think of things that people ask you all the time.

The topics on your content calendar can be all the questions you get asked on a regular basis. My final recommendation is to block off days in your schedule to create content. Doing batch content saves time.

You can sit down for a day or two at a time and create content for the entire month or the quarter so that you're not feeling overwhelmed with trying to create content all the time. If you create at least four videos in one day, you will have content to share once per week for any given month. You can also repurpose each video for various platforms including short and long lengths. Various social media platforms favor short length video content. For example: YouTube Shorts are 60 seconds, TikTok videos are 60 seconds, and Instagram Reels vary from 30, 60, to 90 seconds.

Connect with me. I can help you!

Please visit my website to learn how I can work together to achieve your business goals. **www.qualitymediaconsultants.com** or **www. lorimanns.com**. On social media find me @iamdrlorimanns on Facebook, Instagram, Twitter (**X**), and Threads. Also **search Dr. Lori A. Manns** on YouTube and LinkedIn.

A bit about me and the difference I can make working with you

I'm Lori A. Manns, president of *Quality Media Consultant Group*. We are a consultancy firm specializing in media, marketing, and sales solutions for optimal business growth and scalable success. We help our clients get more sales and more revenue for their bottom line in less time than it would take them on their own.

The results that we help our clients to achieve include; increased revenue, leads, and brand awareness. This results in more clientele and increased sales contributing to growth and optimal success. After working with us, many clients report brand elevation to a point where they now attract their ideal clients and customers on a consistent basis as well as opportunities to be featured in the press. They also report getting more leads, speaking opportunities, and being seen as the expert or authority in their field.

The main difference we help entrepreneurs achieve is increased revenue. With a strategic and magnetic marketing plan, our business owners attract their target market quicker, and more effectively.

My ideal clients are mostly female entrepreneurs who are spiritual, savvy, service-based, purpose-driven, women/business owners who want to either reach six or seven figures in their businesses. These women are accomplished, smart, and have gifts, skills, and talents that they want to use to **earn a living while maximizing their expertise.**

They are their own commodity. I enjoy connecting with women who have spirituality as their foundation and want to connect with others who are like-minded and are **not ashamed to share their spirituality** on their business platform.

What's unique about me as a professional is that I am a spiritual entrepreneur, great storyteller, a word whisperer and people builder. I was **always comfortable saying that I believe in God.** I am 100% willing to put myself out there as a spiritual entrepreneur.

Additionally, I am great at telling stories to help connect with people. I use this skill to teach my clients how to tell their stories and share them authentically and confidently. When I became determined that I was going to use my spirituality and storytelling as part of my brand, I began attracting more women of faith who had stories to tell. Another thing that's different about me is that I like to build people up. I like to build up their confidence and self-esteem to show them that they have unique gifts, skills, and talents. I am very adept at showing people how they can use their talents and skills to make money. I'm a business coach who can find an angle to help someone creatively market and make money from whatever talent or skill they have.

The problems my company helps solve

We specialize in **solving the problem of a lack of clientele** and revenue. We help entrepreneurs and small business owners level up their income so they do not suffer from the feast or famine syndrome. We help them to create a growth strategy and sales plan that results in more revenue on a consistent basis. We teach our clients how to identify a marketing strategy that will magnetically attract their target market and convert prospects into paying customers consistently.

What did you learn from this chapter or this book? Feel free to use the #SheThinksLikeACEO hashtag and let us know. On the two pages following this chapter, you'll be able to record your thoughts and Aha's.

Dr. Lori A. Manns is the founder and president of *Quality Media Consultant Group*, a business consultancy firm specializing in media, marketing, and sales strategies and solutions for small business success. Known as a trailblazing business coach, Manns has career experience in business development, marketing strategy, brand development, and messaging as well as media buying. Ms. Manns holds a bachelor's degree in Mass Communications from Auburn University at Montgomery. In her corporate career, she served as Senior Multi-Media Account Manager for two of the largest broadcast media companies in the USA prior to becoming an entrepreneur. Dr. Manns is an award-winning entrepreneur who has coached hundreds of entrepreneurs toward attaining multiple six and seven figure businesses. Lori hosts national tours, educating entrepreneurs on how to improve sales by attaining sponsorships from corporations. She has a strong passion for philanthropy and enjoys giving back. Lori is the founder and president of *Live Healthy & Thrive Youth Foundation, Inc.*, a 501(c) 3 non-profit organization based in Atlanta. In her spare time, Lori volunteers for several organizations such as Hosea Feed the Hungry & Homeless and Atlanta Mission. She is also regular contributor to Forbes.com. Dr. Lori currently lives in Atlanta, GA.

Website: www.qualitymediaconsultants.com
www.lorimanns.com
Email: info@qualitymediaconsultants.com
Location: Atlanta, Georgia
Facebook: www.facebook.com/iamdrlorimanns
Instagram: www.Instagram.com/iamdrlorimanns
Clubhouse: www.clubhouse.com/iamdrlorimanns
Twitter: www.twitter.com/iamdrLoriManns
Threads: www.threads.net/iamdrLoriManns
Other: www.youtube.com/@LoriAManns

Use this area to journal your thoughts
surrounding your Aha's from this chapter.

Use this area to journal your thoughts surrounding your Aha's from this chapter.

"Your Life is a Gift from God. What You do with it is Your Gift to God."

~Unknown

Go Further Faster, Have Less Stress, And Make More Money

Could you use a boost in your business productivity, state of mind, motivation, and happiness? I bet you could, and I'm sure your sales would increase too!

Being disorganized can negatively impact your productivity by 77%, your state of mind by 65%, your motivation by 54%, and your happiness by 40% (as cited from several sources).

And that's why getting organized in your business is so important and one of the key tools that can help you to get organized, keep focused, and save you time is an online scheduling software.

I'm sure you can relate to forgetting an appointment, not logging an event in your calendar, or playing phone tag back and forth with someone trying to coordinate schedules. Today, especially if you are a service-based business, consultant, or coach, the lifeline of your business is reliant on appointments and meetings. An online scheduling system provides you, your prospects, and your clients with an easy way to book appointments.

Sit back and quickly learn about a technology that can make a difference in your business from Nadine Mullings. Nadine Mullings has over 20 years of experience in marketing and an MBA with an Ecommerce specialization. She works with coaches, consultants, and content creators to attract new clients, get repeat business, and build a strong social network through her proven B.E.S.T. Marketing System™.

Nadine will share how she leveraged scheduling tools and how utilizing them can help you launch, grow, or scale and achieve a greater level of success!

A Conversation with Nadine Mullings

The technology system that I used in my business that has made a world of difference is using **scheduling systems**. Scheduling systems can help you to be more effective and efficient in your business. I use scheduling systems in two ways: the first way is to schedule appointments with my clients. I just send my clients a link, they click on the link, they see what's available in my calendar, and they schedule their appointment. This has been super helpful and has made a big difference in my business.

The second way I use scheduling systems is for my marketing activities. I do a certain amount of activities every month, and I'm consistent in what I do and how I do it. Having technology that helps me to schedule my marketing activities has made a huge difference in my business. I really recommend scheduling systems that help you to schedule your marketing activities like your social media posts and your emails.

What Was Hard Before I Leveraged This Technology

Before using scheduling systems, I felt really overwhelmed. I felt like I wasn't doing things efficiently. When I didn't have a scheduling system, I did a lot of back and forth with my clients and prospects either by email or voice messages to schedule their appointments. I also felt overwhelmed because there are so many different social media platforms, and I'd have to go on all the different platforms to post my social media messages. Using scheduling systems helped me to feel **less overwhelmed and more organized.**

What Changed for Me Implementing This Technology

What specifically changed for me is, things became easier, and more organized. I became more efficient as well, once I started to embrace using scheduling systems for my client appointments and marketing activities.

How I Overcame A Challenging Stage in My Business

In the beginning of my business, I struggled with what to do, when to do it, and how to do it. This can be a key struggle for most new business owners. They're not sure what to do to market their business. They're not sure how to do it consistently or even the frequency they need to be doing it, and they're really not even sure about most of the steps involved.

> **In the beginning of my business, I struggled with what to do, when to do it, and how to do it. This can be a key struggle for most new business owners.**

I struggled with this in the very beginning stages of my business, and what I did to overcome that challenge was to **create a written marketing plan** that I could refer to, that would help me to determine what I needed to be doing, how I needed to be doing it, and when I should be doing it. That really helped to turn my business around because I would always **refer to my marketing plan** and strategy to keep me on track.

Why It's Important to Have A Coach, Consultant, Or Mentor

The three pivotal reasons why every entrepreneur and especially female business owners should work with a coach, a consultant, or a mentor would be, number one, a coach really is there to help guide you and to help map out an actual game plan for your business. I think having a coach is super important to give you that game plan and to guide you and to support you and **keep you accountable.**

I've had a coach from the very beginning of starting my business. The type of coach I've hired and the way that I've worked with coaches has changed, but I do see the importance of having a coach, especially if you're a solopreneur; having that support and accountability is going to be key to growing your business. That's why I think a coach is super important for business owners.

Secondly, a mentor is very similar to a coach, but I consider a mentor to be somebody who's already in your field and is way ahead of you. Having a mentor that **has been there and has done that** can also guide you, but in a different way by telling you what to look out for and what they went through. This can be beneficial and super helpful for you as a business owner.

Thirdly, a consultant. I look at a consultant as somebody that you will hire when you're further along in your business. When you have the funds and ability to hire a consultant, you can hire a consultant that specializes in key areas that can help you build your business. A consultant can be someone like a sales consultant, a financial consultant, or a marketing consultant, and because they specialize in those areas, they can really help you to up-level your business.

> **"When you have the funds and ability to hire a consultant, you can hire a consultant that specializes in key areas that can help you build your business.**

When you work with a consultant, they are able to find blind spots in your business that you are not able to see for yourself. So, I really do think having a consultant can be super beneficial for a business owner. Either way, whether you have a coach, a mentor, or consultant, those are all great options for a female business owner. As a Marketing Mentor/Strategist, I support my clients and keep them accountable for their marketing goals.

How This Technology Will Make A Difference in Your Business

The way that utilizing scheduling systems can dramatically help a woman running a business is saving her time. A lot of women are juggling a lot of things; wearing various hats in the office, in the business, and at home. They're very time-scarce or time-poor, so finding key technologies and systems that help them to get their time back is going to be key.

That's why I highly recommend scheduling systems because scheduling systems can really save you a ton of time and **give you your time back.** Scheduling systems are super affordable and allow you to be effective and efficient. That is why it's important to consider scheduling systems, whether it be for scheduling your client appointments or scheduling your marketing activities.

Why You Should Consider Adding This Technology Platform to Help You Launch, Grow, Or Scale Your Business

Women entrepreneurs and business owners, in general, are struggling to launch, grow, and scale their businesses; that's why it's super important to be efficient and effective. When you're efficient and effective in business, you're more than likely going to stay open and stay in business longer. I reccommend using scheduling systems, whether you're in the launch stage, the growth stage, or the scale stage of your business, because it simplifies your life and allows you to efficiently schedule appointments and effectively schedule your marketing activities.

Challenges I can Help You Avoid

I help my clients avoid being inconsistent with their marketing by helping them to create a plan, schedule, and calendar. I help them with their lack of clarity by getting them clear on who they are called to serve and what their ideal marketing strategy needs to be.

The Benefits of Leveraging This Technology

The challenge that leveraging a scheduling system can alleviate for female entrepreneurs and CEOs or business owners is eliminating the back and forth of scheduling clients. Scheduling systems allow you to book your clients faster, which allows you to get clients faster, which also allows you to make money faster. In addition, when you're using scheduling systems for your marketing activity, it helps you to be consistent.

> **"Scheduling systems allow you to book your clients faster, which allows you to get clients faster, which also allows you to make money faster.**

Without scheduling systems, sometimes you forget to do key marketing activities in your business. Therefore, using a scheduling system for your marketing activity will help you to be consistent; you're able to get more exposure, get more visibility, which always leads to getting more clients if your messaging is clear and if your ideal client is clear.

How You Can Go Further Faster

It's really advantageous for female CEOs and entrepreneurs and business owners, whether they're in the growth stage or scale stage of their business, to work with a marketing mentor /strategist or a marketing agency because, as business owners, you don't know everything, you can't do everything, and you can't specialize in everything. Reaching out to someone who can handle particular araeas of your business and someone who is knowledgeable in certain aspects of your business is advantageous and better for a business owner, especially key aspects like marketing.

A Successful Outcome

I have a client who is a successful insurance agent, but she was really overwhelmed and unclear about how to efficiently and effectively market her business. Because she was so overwhelmed and unclear, she wasn't really seeing the true success that she could have in her business, even though by industry standards she was successful. She needed to alleviate the overwhelm and get clarity on what she needed to do to grow her business. After working with me, we created a 12-month marketing plan and a calendar for her business. After she knew what to do, how to do it, and when to do it, she became clear and consistent, and because of her clarity and consistency, she's now getting new clients on a regular basis through social media.

Things Were Challenging for Me, Too, Until I Leveraged This Technology

As a female entrepreneur and business owner, I struggled with what I should be doing consistently to market my business. Even though I have a marketing background, and I have a marketing degree, I still struggled with what I needed to do to consistently market my business. It was one of the key things that really was a pain point and a challenge for me when I initially started my business.

> **"Even though I have a marketing background, and I have a marketing degree, I still struggled with what I needed to do to consistently market my business.**

A Lesson I learned

One of the most important lessons that I learned early on as an entrepreneur that changed or heavily affected the way I do business is the importance of having support. Many times, when you start a business, you have a vision, you have an idea, you have a dream, and you have a goal, but a lot of the time, it's just you. You are a solopreneur.

You usually don't start off with a big team, so it's important to truly understand that you need support. Thinking about key ways that you can get support? As I mentioned before, look for a coach, look for a mentor, or eventually hire a consultant—all great ways to support your business. However, not only those key things but also having support within your business for implementation.

So, considering things like an assistant or even a virtual assistant can really help you get the support that you need in your business. Also, think about having support from other entrepreneurs and business owners, having things like masterminds where you're able to talk to other people who are in business, and they can give you feedback and ideas.

Masterminds are a great way to really brainstorm with other people who know what you're going through. Another key thing would be having accountability partners, someone that you call on a regular basis that keeps you accountable for the goals that you have in your business.

Questions You Should Ask Yourself . . .

The most important question women should ask themselves as they consider where they are today and where they want to be tomorrow is, "Who do I need to be to get to where I want?" Even though I teach people strategies and how to create a plan, a lot of the time it's not just about the written plan; it's also about who you are internally.

> **"You must think: In order for me to get to the next level in business, who do I really need to be?**

You must think: In order for me to get to the next level in business, **who do I really need to be?** Do I need to be more confident? Do I need to be more assertive? Do I need to be more aggressive? Do I need to be more clear? What are those key adjectives and things that you need to be in order to get to the next level? In order to take your business to the next level, you really have to take yourself to the next level. A lot of business development is actually personal development.

My Recommendation

My recommendation when it comes to technology and using any type of technology or platform is to **not be fearful.** Sometimes technology can be very intimidating, especially when you're new to something, or you've never used it before. I would say be fearless when it comes to technology, and to use whatever's going to make you more efficient and effective in your business. Specifically, when it comes to scheduling tools that are going to make you an effective and efficient entrepreneur. I recommend scheduling tools to help you with scheduling your client appointments and also scheduling tools to help you schedule out your marketing activities. So, don't be intimidated; **be fearless and move forward** with the technology that you need in order to be effective and efficient in your business.

Connect with me. I can help you!

If you would like to learn more about my services at *Nadine Mullings Marketing Agency*, you can go to **nadinemullings.com.** If you would like to use scheduling tools, I definitely recommend the all-inclusive tool **feacreate.com** to schedule appointments and your marketing activity. Need help with your marketing? Get my FREE download, *Discover Two Powerful Ways to Successfully Plan Your Marketing* by going to **nadinemullings.com/power**

A Bit About Me and the Difference I Can Make Working with You

My company is Nadine Mullings Marketing Agency, and we help faith-based Christian women to stop being random and start being specific, strategic, and spirit-led when it comes to their marketing so they can attract their ideal clients and make a bigger impact and income in the world.

I find that one of the biggest problems that people have when it comes to marketing their business is consistency. They struggle to be consistent. They do things and then stop and then start, and staying consistent is really when you're going to see results from your marketing efforts. I help my clients to get all the things in place in order for them to be consistent and get results from their marketing efforts.

> **"I find that one of the biggest problems that people have when it comes to marketing their business is consistency. They struggle to be consistent.**

The outcome that my clients achieve from working with me is fourfold.

First, **they get clarity.** They get clear on **who** they are called to serve. They get clear on their messaging, and they get clear on what they need to be doing to market their business.

The second thing is that **we help them to be consistent** by planning out their marketing, creating a strategy, having a calendar, and having a schedule.

The third thing would be **visibility.** In creating a marketing calendar and being consistent, we teach our clients how to be visible in the marketplace so that people can get to know them and their service or product.

The fourth outcome is, because we help our clients become clear, consistent, and visible, **they get more clients.**

The difference leveraging a scheduling platform makes is, it helps you to be clear, consistent, and visible, so you can get more clients. You'll be **less stressed** and overwhelmed. When you have a plan, a strategy, a calendar, and a schedule, it's easier for you to market your business and service your clients.

My ideal clients are women entrepreneurs and business owners who have service-based businesses and are faith-based Christians, specifically those who are practicing random acts of marketing. They're not very strategic, and they're not being Spirit-led with how they need to market their business.

Several things make me unique and different compared to other marketing agencies and marketing strategists out there. First of all, I'm an award-winning marketer. I've won awards for social media, and I've won awards for content marketing; therefore, I'm definitely knowledgeable in the space of social media and content marketing, but in addition to being an award-winning marketer, my focus really is to help my clients to not only create a marketing strategy but to also be Spirit-led. I want them to tap into the importance of being Spirit-led when it comes to decisions that they need to make to market their business. I think that's different from most marketing agencies or marketing strategists out there. Most agencies and strategists will focus on your marketing strategy and your activities, but they would not focus as much on how you're using your spirit and your intuition to market and promote your business.

> **❝I'm an award-winning marketer. I've won awards for social media, and I've won awards for content marketing; therefore, I'm definitely knowledgeable in the space of social media and content marketing.**

The Problems My Company Helps Solve

I find that most people are not clear about what they need to do. They're not consistent. The problem that my company solves is, I help my clients to get clear, focused, and consistent so that they can get results from their marketing efforts. Results usually look like more clients, more income, and more time.

What did you learn from this chapter or this book? Feel free to use the #SheThinksLikeACEO hashtag and let us know. On the two pages following this chapter, you'll be able to record your thoughts and Aha's.

Nadine Mullings is known as The B.E.S.T. Marketing Strategist™. She is passionate about assisting entrepreneurs and small business owners to market and promote their businesses both online and offline using Spirit-led marketing strategies.

With over 20 years of experience in marketing and an MBA with an Ecommerce specialization, Nadine uses her experience and education to help small business owners to promote their brands using various marketing tools and strategies.

She works with coaches, consultants, and content creators to attract new clients, get repeat business, and build a strong social network through her proven B.E.S.T. Marketing System™.

Website:	www.nadinemullings.com
Email:	nadine@nadinemullings.com
Location:	Fort Lauderdale, FL
Facebook:	www.facebook.com/NadineMulllings
Instagram:	www.instagram.com/iamnadinemullings

Use this area to journal your thoughts surrounding your Aha's from this chapter.

Use this area to journal your thoughts
surrounding your Aha's from this chapter.

"Knowledge is Power!"

~ Thomas Jefferson

Don't Leave Money On The Table While Driving Your Car!

You may be missing out on a large tax refund or not maximizing all the tax deductions available for your business!

According to a 2017 report, manual mileage logging adds an average of 21 administrative hours annually per employee, stated on TaxAct.com. Mileage deduction is an ordinary and necessary business deduction (under section 162 of the Title 26, IRC Code).

As a business owner, freelancer, or entrepreneur, there are tax deductions you can receive each time you use your car for business or administrative purposes.

MileIQ users save around $7,124 per year, making this a great cost-saving app. The app itself is free for up to 40 drives each month.

Without this app, you may be leaving valuable deductions on the table!

No need to worry . . . technology is here! Tracking your business mileage can save you money when you file your taxes. Tina R. Bolden is a tax trainer and tax adviser who loves to coach and train clients. As an Enrolled Agent, Tina is licensed to represent clients in all 50 states, and internationally, for the Internal Revenue Service. Tina has over 15 years of tax consulting and tax advisement experience. She is formerly from Arthur Anderson | tax division. With her advanced tax strategies along with her keen research skills, she unveiled an error that saved her client over $6.2M in tax liabilities. Tina currently focuses on Private Clients in the following industries: real estate investors, legacy entrepreneurs, estate, trust, and fiduciary advising, and women entrepreneurs.

Sit back and quickly learn about a technology app that can make a difference in your business Tina Bolden (or "Ms. Tina," as friends and family call her) will share how using a mileage app for your business can help you launch, grow, or scale, and achieve a greater level of success!

Conversation with Tina R. Bolden, EA, MBA, MST

The technology platform I used that made a difference in my business

The technology app I will discuss is *MileIQ.* This is a secure software backed by Microsoft. As a woman entrepreneur who is no doubt probably wearing many hats, you do not have the time to keep track of your miles, manually. It's a cumbersome task. With *MileIQ*, you no longer need to manually keep track of your mileage. Many business owners do not keep track of their mileage and thus are missing out on valuable federal and state tax deductions.

This mileage app is very straightforward. You can swipe left or right to document a business or personal mileage. A monthly report or YTD can be forwarded to your e-mail. Utilizing this app as a business owner, along with our other technology apps adds value to the client if you're called into an audit.

MileIQ is a great and affordable investment and worth the cost. I have often seen capturing this deduction worth thousands of dollars to a business owner. Keeping track of your mileage is often an overlooked deduction, but proper documentation for this deduction is required by the IRS and state authorities.

We, as part your financial team, evaluate how you will get the best tax benefit. We look at your overall travel, auto repair expenses, etc., to maximize your deductions as a business owner.

When I have represented clients before the IRS and state audits, the main reason for a "disallowed deduction" is lack of proper documentation. *MileIQ* solves the documentation issue and provides the supportive reports required by the IRS and state authorities.

> **"MileIQ solves the documentation issue and provides the supportive reports required by the IRS and state authorities.**

Most taxpayers think, I'll let my Accountant handle that! However, that is a misdirected statement. If you haven't saved the proper records, your accountant, bookkeeper, or wealth adviser will not be able to capture these deductions for you. It's important to note that you, the taxpayer, has the best chance of collecting the proper data immediately or at least within the same year, as opposed to years later, when called into an IRS audit. I recommend clients save all receipts, including oil change receipts, and bank statements to accompany *MileIQ* reports.

What was hard before I leveraged this technology

Early in my career, I felt overwhelmed because I spent a lot of extra time reviewing my clients' documentation and trying to solidify deductions that would help them reduce their overall tax liability. I knew my clients were missing out on valuable deductions because they weren't keeping good mileage records. Now that *MileIQ* is available, I use it, and I recommend it to all my clients.

What changed for me by implementing this technology

Since recommending *MileIQ* to clients, it has helped them to organize and substantiate expense claims. It also helps me to stand up to the IRS and state authorities when necessary. Having my clients use MileIQ has allowed me to focus on doing the work to improve my clients' tax reduction strategies and **increase their profits** instead of spending time trying to organize or help them re-create their deductions. Keeping track of your mileage in an app and providing that information to me saves a lot of time. *MileIQ* has allowed me to take on more clients and still offer technical advice and quality customer service to them. I was able to streamline my operating systems with this technology app.

How I overcame a challenging stage in my business

The challenge that I overcame in my business was not being able to service as many clients as I would have liked because I was spending too much time manually tracking deductions. Once I used *MileIQ* myself and recommended it to my clients, it helped me complete their taxes more efficiently, and it helped them **maximum their tax savings.**

How this technology will make a difference in your business

MileIQ will help you better document your tax write-offs, automate your mileage tracking. You can use it while you are relaxing, so you can swipe, review, and document your acrued mileage easily. Once you have completed this process, you can e-mail the report or upload it to your client portal. It's as easy as that.

It runs in the background while you are multi-tasking and handling your day-to-day business activities. You don't have to worry about turning the app on and off; it's does it for you. There is both a desktop and a mobile app version which you can customize to your preference.

Why you should consider adding this technology platform to help you launch, grow, or scale your business

By using *MileIQ* throughout the year, clients will have better documentation to support their expenses on their tax returns, thus improving their record-keeping while growing their business. This mileage tracking app is an effective source of documentation, along with receipts, bank statements, and other forms of evidence. If the IRS examines any of your tax returns, you may be asked to explain the items reported and provide evidence. A complete set of records will speed up the examination and allow you to work on more important tasks that increase profits and productivity.

How you can go further faster

Using *MileIQ* and working together with our A-plus team of top professionals will help you go further faster. At *Bolden Tax Consulting,* we've completed thousands of tax returns in our combined careers. We are advanced tax strategists with collectively over 30 years of experience, and we can help guide you and offer you pearls of wisdom.

In addition, I have been engaged by auditors, CPAs, attorneys, and other professionals for joint projects. As my client, you will have my impeccable research skills along with access to my ancillary team of professionals in my network. Our team of professionals have trained eyes for what the IRS and other authorities are looking for during an audit, so we are ahead of the game. We are not guessing and hoping the IRS doesn't check your tax returns; we are confident in our work procedures and work ethics. At *Bolden Tax Consulting*, we can help you go further faster while our quality of work will give you peace of mind.

The benefits of leveraging this technology

Using *MileIQ* benefits are as follows:
- It will save you time.
  It is an invaluable resource for record-keeping.
- It may save you thousands of dollars in tax deductions.
- It provides peace of mind that you have sustainable records.
- It is affordable, practicable, and easy to use.

A successful outcome

Barbara Drew, a female entrepreneur, who has been a client for many years, meets me in my Oakland office periodically. I show her how to document her tax-deductible claims on her Annual Tax Organizer. We developed a plan, set up a few templates, and voila! She became an excellent client with great substantive records, and now she teaches other clients to use the *MileIQ* app, along with other invaluable technology apps to substantiate expenses. Making her aware of *MileIQ* allowed her to stop manually keeping her mileage records and embrace technology.

Things were challenging for me, too, until I leveraged this technology

Proper recordkeeping was challenging for me, too, until I leveraged this technology and learned to use it to guide me to better record-keeping and proper documentation. We are often going so fast in life and juggling multiple tasks that we don't want to make the time to document records, but it's worth it, and it's **required by the IRS** for the mileage deduction.

Challenges I can help you avoid

By engaging *Bolden Tax Consulting*, we can help you avoid audits and avoid having insufficient records. The reason clients go to tax professionals is to gain peace of mind and to ensure they have the proper evidence to take a deduction. In addition, we help clients with setting up installment agreements, avoiding tax liens, tax levies, and wage garnishments, etc. We help clients negotiate payments to the IRS, and other authorities. As such, any tax concerns that a client has can be addressed in our firm, from A to Z.

Our clients benefit from our advanced knowledge and experience. We have many years of experience as seasoned Tax Professionals and in representing clients before the IRS with "no-change" audit reports.

The outcome that can be achieved by working with me

We offer clients the peace of mind that their business is being properly addressed in a timely manner. We also provide evidence as necessary. We work smarter to get clients the maximum tax deductions legally possible and increase their profits. As an instructor and consultant, I empower clients with knowledge and train them on how to document for various types of audits and how to be successful entrepreneurs with clean books and records. The best method to protect clients is to help them document their records properly, stay in compliance, and stay on top of all outstanding issues, including tracking their mileage, preferably using great tools like *MileIQ*.

> **"As an instructor and consultant, I empower clients with knowledge and train them on how to document for various types of audits and how to be successful entrepreneurs with clean books and records.**

What's unique about me as a professional that's different from others who offer similar services?

Collectively, as a team, we are customer-focused with proven technical knowledge and skills. My past research and analytical experience is extremely useful to my clients, and I pride myself on providing exceptional customer service. My team and I understand the needs of you, the entrepreneur first-hand. I started my professional career at Arthur Anderson, one of the top International CPA Firms in public accounting and then turned my knowledge and experience into creating a boutique firm. We have been highly trained by the IRS, Arthur Anderson, and Spidell Publishing, and we continue to stay above our competition by exceeding the expectations of our clients with continuous training. We treat our clients like members of our own family.

We have designed our own iron-tough team (CPAs, attorneys, Enrolled Agents, CFPs, etc.) who are excellent resources today and for many years to come. We practice what we preach, and we know what works with our many decades of successful experience.

The problems my company helps solve

We solve our clients' issues with the IRS and state authorities by providing clients with the peace of mind that they are doing the right thing with the proper record-keeping and audit-proof documentation. Peace of mind is priceless. We address clients' IRS correspondence letters (and other authorities) immediately and help relieve them of any anxiety of dealing with the IRS. In addition, we coach our clients to be prepared with substantive documentation during an audit. We offer our clients reliable advice, clear solutions, and excellent customer service that exceeds their expectations.

> **"We address clients' IRS correspondence letters (and other authorities) immediately and help relieve them of any anxiety of dealing with the IRS.**

We also offer tax planning and have years of experience calculating our client's tax liability months in advance. We plan for quarterly estimated tax payments, minimum franchise tax fees, and other regulatory requirements as an entrepreneur or small business owner.

In addition, we also look at our clients' finances held at other institutions (Wealth Management Assets) and offer them private coaching sessions to further minimize tax liabilities on their investments. As a Virtual Tax & Wealth Adviser, I make sure financial statements are accurate and that dollar amounts are properly documented. Our clients walk away with peace of mind knowing that their "affairs are in order and documented." We care about the financial well-being of our clients.

The advantage women entrepreneurs will gain and the difference it can make in their business

As women entrepreneurs, you're constantly juggling the responsibilities of work-life balance. Working with Bolden Tax Consulting, you become part of a successful network of professionals. We make our female entrepreneurs' life less taxing with one-on-one coaching and keeping them connected with various professionals. We make sure that we provide audit-proof documentation, which includes MileIQ. We also maintain and store accurate records digitally on our secured, Amazon-backed client portal. All client records are stored digitally for 4 years, after that, the client has the option to continue with digital storage, if they choose. Many of our small business owners and female entrepreneurs love this service. Digital storage helps them maintain, categorize, and organize their business life cycle. The digital storage serves as a back-up filing system in case clients are ever audited. Clients may need to pull their financial records for various reasons, including fires, earthquakes, or an unforseen world emergency such as the coronavirus. We have your back, but more importantly, we have your records, stored digitally!

I had a client who needed a contract attorney for an emergency issue not related to taxes, and in 10 minutes, I had called one or two of my attorney referrals to address the client's issue the same day. The entrepreneur was appreciative of the resource we were able to provide so she could focus on her business productivity.

A lesson I learned early on as an entrepreneur that changed or heavily affected the way I do business today

I learned early in my career the importance of hiring professional coaches. Initially, I stumbled in my career. I was not reaching my goals seamlessly, but once I hired coaches in different areas of my life, it made a huge difference for me. Now, I was able to develop professionally as well as hone my interpersonal skills. I pride myself on hiring tax & wealth coaches early on, and now I am a Virtual Tax & Wealth Adviser, coach, and mentor. As a serial entrepreneur, I also learned the importance of having a team. Don't do this alone.

> **"Initially, I stumbled in my career. I was not reaching my goals seamlessly, but once I hired coaches in different areas of my life, it made a huge difference.**

The most important question women should ask themselves

Questions you should ask yourself personally: "Am I up to the challenge with the bumps in the road? Do I have the *Black Mamba* mentality, like Kobe Bryant, for my business?" Do you tell yourself: "I will do whatever it takes to succeed, and failure is not an option?" Are you also making sure you continually educate yourself and invest in yourself? This will give you a higher level of confidence.

The questions you should ask yourself professionally: "Am I developing a team of resourceful professionals that will support my current and future business goals?" For example, have you hired or are you looking to hire an accountant, financial advisor, business attorney, banker, etc.?

"Are my current advisors up to date with today's technology and endorse technology and mobile apps, along with online tools such as *Mint, QuickBooks* online, or *MileIQ*?"

Since technology is our future, women entrepreneurs will need to have tax professionals who are willing to grow with their businesses, and that includes growth while embracing technology.

Once you have a respectable, solid team that you trust, your business will be successful for years to come.

Questions you should ask yourself before choosing a tax professional

Does the tax professional have the right licenses, such as an *Enrolled Agent, CPA,* or *LLM* credentials? In addition, is she passionate about her financial profession? Is she a great sounding board for you? Will she help you when you are making financial decisions? Choosing the right tax professional is a long-term investment, an investment in the success of your business.

Unfortunately, in my career, I have seen tax clients engage the improper qualified professional who didn't have the proper tax license or credentials. The IRS was unforgiving to the taxpayer during the audit; the auditor stated, "The Taxpayer should have known the professional didn't have a tax license; the professional's license was not a tax license."

Your investment advisor is not your tax adviser by default. A specific license is required to represent clients before the IRS. We have seasoned professionals in our firm who will represent you before the IRS and those who will represent you in Tax Court.

> **"Unfortunately, in my career, I have seen tax clients engage the improper qualified professional who didn't have the proper tax license or credentials.**

And finally, the client should choose a tax professional that gives them time to review the return prior to e-filing the returns to the IRS. Ultimately, the client, not the tax adviser, is responsible for filing accurate returns.

My Recommendation

My recommendation is to make sure you have your organized documents. I am not just talking about your mileage documentation.

Make sure you have your personal and business financial statements and records in order. Having your documents in order includes having an updated Will or Living Trust, if you are a property owner. Make sure that you have dotted your I's and crossed your T's so that you are in control of your life and your legacy and not caught off guard by an unexpected situation.

Connect with me

You can reach me at Bolden Tax Consulting, and the website is www.boldentax.com. My office phone number is (510) 682-3688. Please use TBOL884A for a 20% discount when downloading the MileIQ app.

What did you learn from this chapter or this book? Feel free to use the #SheThinksLikeACEO hashtag and let us know. On the two pages following this chapter, you'll be able to record your thoughts and Aha's.

Tina Bolden, EA, MBA, MST, is a Virtual Tax & Wealth Advisor. Tina Bolden is the Principal and Virtual Tax & Wealth coach at Bolden Tax Consulting, as well as a Tax Instructor and trainer. She is an enrolled agent and is licensed to represent clients in all 50 states and internationally before the Internal Revenue Service. Her most recent accomplishments has been unveiling an error that saved her publicly traded client over $6.2M in tax liabilities. She holds dual master degrees; Masters in Taxation and an MBA. In addition, Tina is a graduate of JFK University, Institute of Entrepreneurial Leadership Program with Dr. Deju and his leadership team.

Tina is also the Founding President and now Executive Director of "The Pearls of Wisdom, Inc.," a not-for-profit 501(c)(3) organization.

Website:	www.boldentaxconsulting.com
Email:	tbolden@boldentax.com
Location:	California
Facebook:	www.facebook.com/BoldenTaxConsulting
Twitter:	www.twitter.com/ConsultMsTina
LinkedIN:	www.linkedin.com/company/bolden-tax-consulting
Instagram:	www.instagram.com/boldentaxconsulting
Pinterest:	www.pinterest.com/BoldenTaxConsulting

Use this area to journal your thoughts surrounding your Aha's from this chapter.

**Use this area to journal your thoughts
surrounding your Aha's from this chapter.**

Thank you for choosing this book!

Be sure to access your FREE gifts to assist you with
Thinking Like a CEO.

Thank You for Reading

Please share your thoughts and reactions.

Recommended Reading

UN-Market Your Business: 10 Ways for Savvy Entrepreneurs to Stand Out, Stop Struggling, & Start Profiting

UN-Market Your Business is the breakout business book filled with real, effective, small business marketing strategies that savvy entrepreneurs have been waiting for.

You started your business, struggled longer than necessary, and finally got your mojo going. Now it's time to step on the gas and grow.

90-Day Gratitude Journal for Your Business: The Purpose-Driven Entrepreneur's Guide to Gratitude – in a few minutes each day

The 90-Day Gratitude Journal for Your Business focuses on the practice of gratitude and being grateful for everything your business has manifested for you.

One, simple prompt guides you thoughtfully each day to reflect and appreciate all the goodness your business brings forth.

The B. E. S. T. Marketing Planner: A 90 Day Guide to Help You Master Your Marketing and Grow Your Business

When it comes to marketing your business, are you unsure where to start, inconsistent, or feel overwhelmed?This planner was designed to help you stay on track, get clarity, and organize your business for success, so you can confidently GROW your business!

Purpose Driven Entrepreneur Daily Prayer Journal: Strengthen your Business and Connection with God through the Power of Prayer

As Christians, Believers, and Purpose Driven Entrepreneurs of Faith, prayer is important, purposeful, and a necessity of life.

Have you ever felt that maybe God wasn't listening to your prayers?

Now, you have the opportunity to keep a record of what you're praying for. When your prayers are answered, you can rejoice instead of wonder.

Divine Downloads Loriology: 33 Lessons on Life, Love & Leadership is a collection of 33 insightful and original revelations from entrepreneur and philanthropist Lori A Manns. This book is designed to help you reach your purpose, fulfill your divine destiny and inspire you to achieve the full potential of all that you were created to be, do and have. Sometimes life hinders us from accomplishing our goals and God given assignments.

90-Day Planner for the UN-Intentional Entrepreneur

Your entrepreneurial success is just 90 days away! Whether you're an aspiring entrepreneur or have an established business, this planner will direct you HOW to create the business you've always wanted.

This is NOT your average, run-of-the-mill business planner. You'll be guided every step of the way with structure and accountability. Use the daily, writable pages to help you complete tasks and gain focus.

This planner is a hybrid guided journal and business planner in one. It is designed to lead you where you need to be and where you thought you might never be.

The Ultimate Sales Planner For The Master Closer

Want to achieve your sales goals? Whether you're a sales person, a small business owner, a real estate agent, or an entrepreneur, the secret to achieving your sales goals is being organized. But, how do you become organized? That's where the Ultimate Sales Planner for Master Closers come in. This planner was created by a Master Closer with decades of experience teaching sales professional his rock solid sales methodology.

Technology Resources

Books

- **Believe Bigger** by *Marshawn Evans Daniels*
- **In the Plex:** How Google Thinks, Works, and Shapes Our Lives by *Steven Levy*
- **Prediction Machines:** The Simple Economics of Artificial Intelligence by *Ajay Agrawal, Joshua Gans and Avi Goldfarb*
- **Purpose Driven Lif**e by *Rick Warren*
- **Race After Technology:** Abolitionist Tools for the New Jim Code by *Ruha Benjamin*
- **The AI Advantage:** How to Put the Artificial Intelligence Revolution to Work by *Thomas H. Davenport*
- **The E-Myth** by *Michael Gerber*
- **Think and Grow Rich** by *Napoleon Hill*
- **Video Marketing Strategy:** Harness the Power of Online Video to Drive Brand Growth by *Jon Mowat*
- **Viewership:** The Video Marketing Formula to Get Millions of Views on YouTube by *Adam LoDolce*

Finance/Budgeting

- Cashmapapp.com

Photo/Video

- **Canva:** A free-to-use online graphic design tool. Use it to create social media posts, presentations, posters, videos, logos and more. **nadinemullings.com/canva**
- **Bonjoro:** Send quick personal videos to new leads and customers, to stand out, build trust, and make more sales. **Csicorporation.com/bonjoro**
- **Remini.ai** - AI Photo Enhancer
- **StreamYard:** A professional live streaming and recording studio in your browser. Interview guests, brand your broadcast, and much more. Stream to Facebook, YouTube, LinkedIn, and even Instagram. **Csicorporation.com/streamyard**
- **TubeBuddy:** Accelerate the Growth of Your Audience and Achieve Your Dreams of Becoming a YouTuber. TubeBuddy is the #1 Rated YouTube Video Optimization and Management Toolkit. Free to Install. Bulk Update your Videos. Rank Higher in Search. Optimize Video Tags. **Csicorporation.com/tubebuddy**
- **Vimeo.com:** A start-to-finish video platform giving creative professionals, businesses and organizations everything they need to make and market amazing, impactful videos.

CRM

- **FEA Create:** An all-in-one platform that empowers women to run their online businesses with ease and style including calendar scheduling, websites, emails, courses, funnels, social media, and more. **nadinemullings.com/feacreate**

Communication

- **Zoom:** A unified communication and collaboration platform. Make meaningful connections with meetings, team chat, whiteboard, phone, and more in one offering. **nadinemullings.com/zoom**

SEO

- **KeySearch:** You can do in-depth competition analysis lightning fast and with a push of a button. Just put in a seed keyword and Key Search will return hundreds of related keywords. New features and updates. Your SEO in Another Level. Overtake Your Competition. **Csicorporation.com/keysearch**

Web Design/Landing Pages

- **Elementor:** the leading website builder platform and landing page creator for professionals, coaches, and VAs on WordPress. **Csicorporation.com/elementor**

Productivity

- **Otter.ai:** uses AI to write automatic meeting notes with real-time transcription, recorded audio, automated slide capture, and automated meeting summaries. **Csicorporation.com/otter**
- **RePurpose.io:** Repurposing content for social media made easy. Automatically repurpose YouTube, TikTok, Lives, Podcasts, and Zoom calls. **Csicorporation.com/rp**
- **Sanebox:** Helps your inbox to stay organized and effortlessly clear out years of old emails. **nadinemullings.com/sanebox**
- **Simple Podcast Press:** Simple, elegant and speedy, Simple Podcast Press is a player that gives listeners the opportunity to get much more involved with your show over and above simply listening. **Csicorporation.com/spp**

Other Resources

- https://lorimanns.wearelegalshield.com
- https://10000.cards.com/card/lori-a-manns

Facebook Groups

- **UN-Market Your Business:** Discover how to market your business successfully with your website, your book, and your online strategy.
https://www.facebook.com/groups/unmarketyourbusiness

- **Trailblazer Entrepreneur Nation:** A tribe for trailblazing entrepreneurs who market, sell & serve.™ This group will serve as a community where women and a few good men will share the many demands, struggles and triumphs of entrepreneurship.
https://www.facebook.com/groups/389333151262937

- **Women Faith and Business:** If you are a woman of faith in business, then this group is for you! The goal of the group is to have an open and honest conversation about faith and business. The goal of the group is to
  1. Encourage
  2. Educate
  3. Support
https://www.facebook.com/groups/436724849673829

- **The Closing Academy - Prospect, Close, Repeat:** This group is dedicated to the sales professionals that need or want help with sales. Sales is a teachable skill!! There are resources and experts in this group that are here to help you grow. We want this to be a safe space where you can ask questions and get answers that will help you increase your sales and your ability to close the sale.
https://www.facebook.com/groups/423832065095017

- **Small Business Saturday Shout-out with Alicia Couri:** Each Saturday we will profile 2 Small Businesses. If you want an opportunity to share your business or event coming up, email us support@aliciacouri.com to get on our calendar so we can highlight you!
https://www.facebook.com/groups/sbsso

- **Sista ~ Sista:** We are a community of Women empowering women to bridge the gap and be imperfectly perfect in their life's journey. Be comfortable in your skin... Here's where Queens straighten each other's crown.
https://www.facebook.com/groups/sista.sista.nlc

www.ingramcontent.com/pod-product-compliance
Lightning Source LLC
LaVergne TN
LVHW051703050326
832903LV00032B/3982